52
Heart Lifters
for Difficult
Times

DIANA SAVAGE

Diana Savage

HARVEST HOUSE PUBLISHERS
EUGENE, OREGON

Cover by Koechel Peterson & Associates, Inc., Minneapolis, Minnesota

Cover photos © iStockphoto / Thinkstock

52 HEART LIFTERS FOR DIFFICULT TIMES
Copyright © 2014 by Diana Savage
Published by Harvest House Publishers
Eugene, Oregon 97402
www.harvesthousepublishers.com

Library of Congress Cataloging-in-Publication Data
   Savage, Diana, 1950-
   52 heart lifters for difficult times / Diana Savage.
      pages cm
   ISBN 978-0-7369-5660-4 (pbk.)
   ISBN 978-0-7369-5661-1 (eBook)
   1. Christian life—Meditations. 2. Consolation—Meditations. 3. Encouragement—Religious aspects—Meditations. I. Title. II. Title: Fifty-two heart lifters for difficult times.
   BV4501.3.S2835 2014
   242'.4—dc23
                                  2013016745

This book is dedicated to the dozen or so members of a loosely knit support group divinely assembled during one of the darkest times in my life. You know who you are, although you might not be aware of the identity of the other members. All of you contributed important buoyancy to keep my nose above water. You prayed. You listened. You shared and sympathized appropriately. You gave of your time, energy, and even financial resources on occasion.

I was able write this book because of your loving friendship and support. I am forever grateful.

Contents

What Is a Heart Lifter?

A heart lifter is a smile, a chortle, a glimpse of a blessing. It's a reminder we're not alone on life's journey. It's the assurance that we can count on fellow survivors to show us the route they've charted to better places.

Scott Adams, creator of the *Dilbert* comic strip, claims that no matter how many times he visits New York City, he's always struck by the same thing—a yellow taxicab. That's pretty much a description of what happens in life, isn't it? There seem to be two kinds of people in this world: those who have experienced difficult times and those who are about to.

Often we describe our reaction to setbacks by saying we feel as if we've been run over by a truck. Or maybe someone threw us under the bus. I took years to understand that the way I choose to perceive such experiences determines my chances of emotional and spiritual recovery.

I heard about a woman who was helping her grandchildren craft figures from modeling clay. The four-year-old girl made a recognizable dog, but the grandmother had trouble identifying what her three-year-old grandson had shaped. So she asked him.

He replied, "It's a cat, but a truck ran over it."

A while later, the little girl formed another animal shape while her brother produced another flat slab. The grandma asked him, "What happened to this animal?"

He shrugged. "Same truck."

Don't you hate being knocked down again and again by the same truck? The good news is, we aren't helpless in averting such dangers. It may take practice, but eventually we can learn to identify the sound of approaching trucks and jump out of the way. Or we can avoid the street altogether and remain on the sidewalk. Of course, then we may have to be alert for the sound of flowerpots falling from upper-story windows, but at least we would have made some progress. And even when we're blindsided, focusing on the love and support available from God and fellow believers helps us get back on our feet and resume the journey.

To assist you in that process, these meditations are arranged in four parts.

> *Part One: Choosing Our Outlook.* What we allow our minds to dwell on ultimately determines our destiny.

> *Part Two: Living Miraculously.* To experience the miraculous, we must believe not only that God has the power to perform miracles in our lives but also that he wants to.

> *Part Three: Participating Joyfully.* When we realize God always has our best interests at heart, we can live life with gusto.

> *Part Four: Pursuing Possibilities.* Going after new possibilities in life, regardless of what we've been through, is an important part of God's wonderful plan for us.

These heart lifters are the result of encouragement I have received from others in times of need. Now I'm passing it on to you. My hope is that this book will provide chuckles and cheer, along with insights and inspiration, to help you return to full mobility after being struck by life's yellow taxicabs.

~ Diana Savage

PART ONE
Choosing Our Outlook

Humorist Jay Trachman has pointed out that the formula for a happy marriage is the same as the one for living in California. When you find a fault, don't dwell on it.

That's a good strategy for life in general. God gives each of us the power to choose either the positive or the negative. We can opt for cleanliness or clutter, acceptance or rejection, life or death.

The focus we adopt impacts our self-talk. Our mindset determines whether we cling to encumbrances or dump such baggage for good. Our thoughts and speech patterns affect the way we respond to everything and everyone around us.

It can be frightening and yet positively liberating to realize that what we allow our minds to dwell on ultimately determines our destiny. Our outlook is a key factor in our success.

So let's choose wisely, not only in California but also in any other spot on the planet.

1

Choosing Life, Even If You're Not a Centenarian

I have set before you life and death, blessings and curses.
Now choose life, so that you and your children may live.

DEUTERONOMY 30:19

At a birthday party for a man who had turned 102, he was asked if he thought he would live long enough to enjoy his next birthday celebration. "I certainly do," he replied. "According to statistics, very few people die between the ages of 102 and 103."

I love being around positive people, especially at the beginning of the year, because January is a month of bereavement for me. Every time it rolls around, I must endure the anniversaries of the deaths of my father, mother-in-law, grandfather, and grandmother, as well as the end of a long-term relationship. Coupled with January's long nights and short days, sometimes I struggle with depression. The more I dwell on my losses, the sadder I become.

However, the book of Deuteronomy always turns me around. After reading what might seem like a mind-numbing list of obscure regulations, I come to the passage where the Israelites are given power to choose either life and prosperity or death and adversity. The choice was totally up to them. We have the same option today. While curses and death are always before us, God urges us to reject them in favor of blessings and life.

When Jesus confronted the Pharisees for opposing him at every turn, he used a metaphor he knew his listeners could identify with:

I am the Gate for the sheep. All those others are up to no good—sheep stealers, every one of them. But the sheep didn't listen to them. I am the Gate. Anyone who goes through me will be cared for—will freely go in and out, and find pasture. A thief is only there to steal and kill and destroy. I came so they can have real and eternal life, more and better life than they ever dreamed of (John 10:7-10 MSG).

The thief Death comes to steal, kill, and destroy. Our Redeemer Jesus Christ comes to give us life, both now and forever. We can't even begin to imagine how much better that life is in both quality and quantity.

I love serving a God who wants us always to choose life. When I make the conscious decision to do so, death anniversaries fade in my mind and I remember some of my January blessings, such as the birthdays of my mother and my niece—both wonderful occasions to celebrate.

January is also when God spreads before us 12 new months to enjoy his blessings. Since the choice is up to us, let's select wisely. I'm sure people who do so live longer, happier lives.

At the very least, statistics show that few of those people will die between the ages of 102 and 103.

*Lord, thank you for the wonderful gifts of blessings
and life. I choose them with gratitude for as many
years as you give me on this earth. Amen.*

2

A Rooftop Epiphany

When King Herod heard this he was disturbed, and...
he asked them where the Messiah was to be born.

MATTHEW 2:3-4

Preschoolers visiting a library gathered for story time. After the librarian finished the first page of *There Was an Old Lady Who Swallowed a Fly*, she asked the children, "Do you think she'll die?"

"No," said a little boy in the back. "I saw this last week on *Fear Factor*."

It seems most people are afraid of something. For instance, trepidatious friends of mine worry every time I climb on the roof to hang Christmas lights. But I figure that nearing retirement age is no reason to stay on the ground—as long as I wear sturdy work boots and carry a cell phone in my pocket.

It's also fun waving to startled neighbors while I drape icicle lights from the eaves. I'm never in a hurry to take the lights down, so my house twinkles with Christmas cheer well into the first week of January even though store displays of holiday decorations have already been replaced by valentines.

But before Valentine's Day comes Epiphany, the church festival on January 6. As I climb the ladder that day to unhook light strands, I ponder the message of Epiphany—our loving God taking on human form to redeem us from the clutches of the enemy. Specifically, the festival celebrates the coming of gift-bearing Wise Men who worshiped the baby Jesus as King. It occurs to me that the day is a perfect blending of the two holidays that bookend it—Christmas, a reminder of God's amazing gift, and Valentine's Day, a reminder of God's amazing love.

As I stand on the roof, neighbors across the street see me and wave. In their native Mexico, they customarily celebrate Epiphany, or Three Kings' Day, with *rosca de reyes*. This sweet bread is decorated with candied fruit, and inside the dough is hidden a plastic figurine of baby Jesus to symbolize the infant's need to hide from murderous King Herod.

From the moment of Christ's birth until the day he died, our Lord was the target of prejudice and irrational fear. If government rulers weren't trying to do him harm, religious leaders were out to get him. No wonder he has such great compassion for everyone who suffers today from mistreatment.

After Jesus ascended into heaven, the apostle Peter's epiphanous rooftop vision helped Peter overcome prejudice and understand that God's great gift is for everyone.

> Peter fairly exploded with his good news: "It's God's own truth, nothing could be plainer: God plays no favorites! It makes no difference who you are or where you're from—if you want God and are ready to do as he says, the door is open" (Acts 10:34-35 MSG).

I'm glad the door is wide open, no matter what our social status, bank balance, or nationality may be. This equal footing before God means we can pray with confidence, knowing our heavenly Father is eager to listen to us. That knowledge can also give us courage to face all kinds of difficulties. Even if we're on *Fear Factor*.

Lord Jesus, grant me wisdom to embrace the
epiphany that you don't play favorites, but instead,
you love everyone—equally and unconditionally.
Thank you for such amazing love. Amen.

3

Dragging Around Encumbrances

Let us strip off and throw aside every
encumbrance (unnecessary weight).

Hebrews 12:1 amp

There's nothing like a rummage sale to make you realize how much rummage you already possess. When I stopped by a sale at a local church recently, I was shocked to see all the items that looked exactly like ones cluttering my own home.

Take the well-used electric meat slicer, for instance, or the rubberized jar opener, the white plastic pie carrier, or the rectangular celery keeper in the same shade of green as the empty one on my pantry shelf. I could have sworn the pasta maker in its original box was one I'd sold at my own garage sale a few years before. Doilies, tablecloths, and bedding, exactly like linens in my own closet, mounded colorfully on a long table. An avocado-green salad bowl, identical to a glass bowl I received at my bridal shower in 1972, was marked $8. Seeing all the items for sale reminded me how my own possessions became encumbrances a few years ago when I had to pack them up and haul them to a new house.

The Bible offers us insight concerning encumbrances:

> Therefore, since we are surrounded by such a great cloud of witnesses, let us throw off everything that hinders and the sin that so easily entangles. And let us run with perseverance the race marked out for us...so that [we] will not grow weary and lose heart (Hebrews 12:1,3).

Christian counselor Dr. Gregory L. Jantz talks about finding freedom from what he calls "negative internal messages." In his book *Happy for the Rest of Your Life: Four Steps to Contentment, Hope, and Joy—and the Three Keys to Staying There,* he defines negative internal messages as the messages we've heard, impressions and impacts we've assimilated, and conclusions we've reached over the course of our lives.

> God never intended for you to have your mind filled with negative, destructive messages created through the damage of others. For every lie these messages spew, He holds fast with His truth. His truth is positive, uplifting, empowering, and refreshing. God knows every negative thing you say to yourself; He hears the words of despair you utter and offers words of encouragement instead.[1]

Nearly every person I know carries encumbrances in the form of some sort of emotional bruising and scarring. Our response to these injuries determines our future. If we don't unload the negative baggage, it will become too heavy for us, and we'll stumble under its weight.

That baggage is also uglier than a 42-year-old, avocado-green bowl. Let's get rid of it for good.

Lord Jesus, help me to let go of everything in my life that weighs me down—clutter, resentments, unhealed wounds...all of it. Then let me feel your energizing power as I run life's race unencumbered. Amen.

4

God's Mysterious—and Sometimes Humorous—Ways

Stop and consider God's wonders.

JOB 37:14

After my mother and I went on a cruise sponsored by a famous ministry duo, I sold an article about the experience to a magazine. The editor called back later to say he wanted to purchase the photo I'd sent of Mom posing with the famous couple. "But we need permission to use it. Can you get a release?"

I called the ministry's management group several times but could reach only voicemail. No one returned my messages. Finally I prayed, "Lord, help me connect with the right person," and dialed once again.

This time, instead of a recorded message, it sounded as if the connection opened. I could hear people talking in the background and a voice shouting something like, "Leave me alone!"

More than puzzled, I offered a tentative "Hello?"

A flustered young voice belonging to the vice president's assistant came on the line. She thought she'd punched the forward button but had hit speaker instead. Embarrassed that I'd heard her outburst, she was eager to help. Within the hour I had the permission I needed.

God moves in a mysterious way, his wonders to perform.

That famous phrase comes from "God Moves in a Mysterious Way" by British poet and hymnist William Cowper (1731–1800).

Throughout his life, Cowper struggled with doubt, depression, and fear, yet he declared what he knew to be true about God.

> God moves in a mysterious way,
> His wonders to perform;
> He plants his footsteps in the sea,
> And rides upon the storm.

By the third stanza, Cowper zeroed in on his encouraging point:

> Ye fearful saints, fresh courage take,
> The clouds ye so much dread
> Are big with mercy, and shall break
> In blessings on your head.

When dark clouds gather overhead, it can be difficult to believe that instead of dodging lightning bolts, perhaps I'll be delighting in showers of merciful blessings. Those blessings may include a few lighthearted moments as God uses the foibles of administrative assistants to open doors for me.

Thank you, William Cowper, for continuing to encourage us 200 years after your lifetime. May we similarly inspire others every time we hit our own speaker buttons.

Gracious God, help me to anticipate blessings
instead of always dreading the worst. You do,
indeed, move in mysterious—and even humorous—
ways in my life. I am grateful. Amen.

5

Who Is God's Interpreter?

Who is wise enough to understand this?
Who has been instructed by the LORD and can explain it?

JEREMIAH 9:12

The Lord will carry out his purpose.

JEREMIAH 51:12

On his way to work one day, a professor stopped by the university's cafeteria as rain began to fall. When he got up to leave, he forgot he hadn't brought an umbrella and absentmindedly reached for the nearest one. "That's *my* umbrella," a woman near him said, scowling.

Chagrined at his mistake, the professor hurried on. By the time he reached his office, he was drenched. Then he discovered three umbrellas he'd left in the office over the past several months. He decided to bring them home when he left for the day.

En route to his car, he ran into the same woman who had scolded him. When she spied the umbrellas, she said tartly, "Well, you did real well for yourself today, didn't you?"

Have you ever been judged? When we look again at William Cowper's famous poem "God Moves in a Mysterious Way," we're reminded we shouldn't judge God.

You mean someone would dare do that? Oh, yes. Many of us judge God when we're terrified, hurt, frustrated, or confused. We simply don't understand why he allows magnitude 9.0 earthquakes, three-story tsunamis, levee-breaching rivers, monster tornadoes and hurricanes, omnivorous wildfires, or deadly heat waves. We're stymied when pirates hijack ships or terrorists bomb skyscrapers or insane rulers shanghai children to fight wars. And don't even bring up the subject of the growing sex-slave trade. "Where is God?" we demand to know.

The 1700s—when this poem was penned—were also full of injustice. Cowper's admonishment to his contemporaries is as up-to-date today as it was then. In his poem's later stanzas Cowper declares,

> Judge not the Lord by feeble sense,
> But trust him for his grace;
> Behind a frowning providence,
> He hides a smiling face.

Having encountered that frowning providence, I sometimes wonder if I'll ever see God's smiling face again. My feeble senses, weakened by early teaching about God's harshness and impossible demands, sometimes find it difficult to believe our heavenly Father is concerned for his creation. Acquainted with that feeling in his own life, Cowper continues.

> His purposes will ripen fast,
> Unfolding every hour;
> The bud may have a bitter taste,
> But sweet will be the flower.

Okay. I've experienced green fruit's bitterness and, with a puckered face, wished I'd waited until it ripened. I see where Cowper is going with this.

> Blind unbelief is sure to err,
> And scan his work in vain;
> God is his own interpreter,
> And he will make it plain.

God is his own interpreter. When will I grasp that? With each new bitter experience, I learn just a little more about patiently waiting for the fullness of God's time. That knowledge can serve as an umbrella of comfort in seasons of dripping despair.

And I'll never be scolded for seeking its refuge.

Almighty God, thank you for using a long-dead
poet to remind me not to jump to conclusions
about your ways and your timing. Amen.

In the Shadow of Tradition

You have let go of the commands of God and
are holding on to human traditions.

MARK 7:8

A woman lamented her family's lack of holiday rituals. "We don't have any traditions," she bemoaned. "We just do the same thing year after year after year."

As a child, I saw newscasters reporting on whether a groundhog had seen its shadow on February 2. I wondered who cared and how an underground rodent could possibly predict the remaining number of weeks until spring. It seemed to me like a very peculiar tradition.

Years later I discovered that Groundhog Day began as a Pennsylvania German custom rooted in ancient European weather lore. Continuing the ritual each year—for fun rather than functional forecasting—thousands of people gather at various spots in North America to discover if a groundhog will observe its shadow.

In the United States, Gobbler's Knob in Punxsutawney, Pennsylvania, is the official location. An entire festival has developed around the spring-forecasting event. Attendees enjoy ice-carving exhibitions, trivia contests, the Prognosticators Ball, a chili cook-off, Groundhog Day weddings, sleigh rides, woodchuck whittling, music, and other activities, including the Phil Phind Scavenger Hunt.

Tradition can be a strong element in society, whether whimsical or truly meaningful. While many of our traditions help stabilize society and give balance to our lives, we must guard against allowing tradition to supersede God's laws. If we don't give top priority to God's actual commands, we'll end up in trouble.

In the 1993 comedy film *Groundhog Day*, Bill Murray plays the character of Phil Connors, an egocentric Pittsburgh TV weatherman whose priorities are clearly askew. While covering the annual Groundhog Day event in Punxsutawney, Phil becomes trapped in a never-ending cycle of repeating February 2.

His friend Rita asks how he can know so much about her when they've just met. He replies, "I told you. I wake up every day, right here, right in Punxsutawney, and it's always February second, and there's nothing I can do about it."

In the real world, being bound by human laws can make a person feel trapped. The apostle Paul warned believers in Colossae, "See to it that no one takes you captive through hollow and deceptive philosophy, *which depends on human tradition* and the elemental spiritual forces of this world rather than on Christ" (Colossians 2:8).

God's authentic commands, on the other hand, give life and freedom. The psalmist expressed it this way:

> I reach out for your commands, which I love,
>   that I may meditate on your decrees.
> Remember your word to your servant,
>   for you have given me hope.
> My comfort in my suffering is this:
>   Your promise preserves my life (Psalm 119:48-50).

Eugene Peterson paraphrases that last line, "Your promises rejuvenate me." I love how embracing God's Word results in rejuvenation.

After Punxsutawney Phil retreats to his burrow this year, why don't we think about what governs our lives—God's precepts or mere human rules? Adopting a spiritual self-examination ritual every February 2 is, in my opinion, a much better use of our time than spying on Pennsylvanian groundhogs.

Lord, reveal to me whenever I'm following human
tradition instead of your life-giving instruction. Amen.

The *Rs* of Important Pronunciations

Set a guard over my mouth, LORD;
keep watch over the door of my lips.

PSALM 141:3

Even though the road sign clearly proclaimed, "No left turn Monday thru Friday," a motorist turned left anyway. A nearby police officer sounded his siren and pulled the man over.

"You can't give me a ticket," the driver said.

"I can't?" the officer asked. "Why not?"

"Because it's Wednesday."

"What difference does that make?"

"Look," the driver said as he pointed at the sign. "It says, 'No left turn Monday, *Thrusday*, and Friday'!"

It's strange how difficult pronouncing phrases with *r* in them can be, such as "I'm sorry," "I was wrong," or "Will you forgive me?" Tongues also trip when rash promises are uttered, secrets are spilled, or accusations are made.

The apostle James warns about the dangers of unguarded speech.

> A word out of your mouth may seem of no account, but it can accomplish nearly anything—or destroy it!

> It only takes a spark, remember, to set off a forest fire. A careless or wrongly placed word out of your mouth can do that. By our speech we can ruin the world, turn harmony to chaos, throw mud on a reputation, send the whole world up in smoke and go up in smoke with it, smoke right from the pit of hell.

> This is scary: You can tame a tiger, but you can't tame a
> tongue—it's never been done. The tongue runs wild, a
> wanton killer (James 3:5-8 MSG).

Scary indeed! I'm no tiger tamer, so how can I hope to control my own tongue? Fortunately, God never commands us to do anything he does not empower us to carry out. So when Paul writes, "Do not let any unwholesome talk come out of your mouths, but only what is helpful for building others up according to their needs, that it may benefit those who listen" (Ephesians 4:29), we can draw on God's supernatural help to follow that command.

I don't know of anyone who hasn't been wounded in one way or another by someone's careless talk. Acid accusations, cutting criticisms, and other wild words leave their marks on our memories. It usually takes a lot of work to forgive the taloned tongues that shred our self-esteem into quivering ribbons.

By comparison, mispronouncing a day of the week seems quite innocuous. But we can use the mispronunciation as a reminder to ask for God's help in monitoring everything we say—from *R*s, to arguments, to truly edifying speech.

Even on Thrusdays.

> *Dear Lord, set a guard over my mouth so I may*
> *speak only that which is helpful to others. And I*
> *pray for the grace to forgive those who are not*
> *as careful about what they say to me. Amen.*

Like...Fantasy Football Games

Let us love one another, for love comes from God.

1 JOHN 4:7

Kailey and her husband, Jared, usually gave each other gifts on Valentine's Day, but after a downturn in the economy, they decided to forego presents and simply tell each other what they would give if they had the money to spend.

Kailey told Jared her fantasy present to him would be tickets to a University of Washington football game, including an overnight stay in Seattle so they could return to some of the places they'd visited when they were dating. Then she gazed into Jared's eyes and asked what his gift to her would be.

After a long pause, he said, "Well, you could come with me."

Most lovers are more romantic than poor Jared. The Greeting Card Association estimates that approximately one billion valentines are mailed worldwide each year. That makes Valentine's Day second only to Christmas as the largest card-sending holiday.

Sending valentines is not the only way to express our love for others. Actions are also important. God uses both words and actions to communicate his love for his children. The apostle John explains that God showed his love to us by sending "his one and only Son into the world that we might live through him" (1 John 4:9).

While being affectionate toward someone on a valentine list isn't difficult, exhibiting a loving attitude toward a contrary in-law, a hard-to-please boss, or neighbors with yippy dogs might not be as easy. Yet compared to the loving sacrifice God made on our behalf, it's really no sacrifice at all to show love to everyone around us.

The apostle Paul wrote to the church at Galatia, "Serve one another humbly in love. For the entire law is fulfilled in keeping this one command: 'Love your neighbor as yourself'" (Galatians 5:13-14). He also urged believers in Rome, Corinth, Galatia, Ephesus, Philippi, Colossae, and Thessalonica to love and serve one another.[1] Other apostles encouraged Christians to do the same.[2]

All three of the short epistles written by the apostle John carry that theme,[3] such as this admonition: "My dear children, let's not just talk about love; let's practice real love" (1 John 3:18 MSG).

The evidence is clear that while Valentine's Day is named for Saint Valentine, the holiday actually originated with God. So let's think of February 14 as God's Day and consider those who might benefit from our loving words *and* deeds—whether or not fantasy football games are involved.

Lord, help me show love to everyone you
send across my path today. Amen.

Courage, Strength, and Memorials That Rock

These stones are to be a memorial to the people of Israel forever.

JOSHUA 4:7

According to playwright Gore Vidal, Ronald Reagan was considered in 1959 for the lead role of a distinguished front-running presidential candidate in Vidal's play *The Best Man*. However, Reagan didn't end up with the part because he seemed to lack the "presidential look."

After he was elected at age 69 to the office of president of the United States—despite his "unpresidential" looks—Reagan often joked about his advanced years. He particularly loved a quote attributed to Thomas Jefferson. "He said that we should never judge a president by his age, only by his work. And ever since he told me that, I've stopped worrying," quipped Reagan. "And just to show you how youthful I am, I intend to campaign in all 13 states."

Since serving as our fortieth president, President Reagan received many honors, not only in this country but also around the world. Hospitals, schools, roads, parks, squares, airports, buildings, institutions, and even an aircraft carrier bear his name.

Many of our US presidents have been honored with memorials. Every year on the federal holiday of President's Day, most states celebrate two presidents in particular: George Washington and Abraham Lincoln. It's safe to say these fine men weren't more intelligent, more capable, or wiser than all the other presidents. They're more famous, perhaps, because they led our country during times of national crises by modeling strength and courage.

When God rescued the people of Israel in critical times, he often instructed them to erect memorials. To be sure, those memorials were mere rock piles instead of enormous statues or needle-like towers. But they served as reminders that Yahweh was a God of power and deliverance.

After Moses died, Israel's new leader, Joshua, faced the daunting task of turning millions of desert nomads into warriors capable of invading and possessing the Promised Land. God knew Joshua needed encouragement. "Be strong and courageous, because you will lead these people," God told him. "Be strong and very courageous...Have I not commanded you? Be strong and courageous" (Joshua 1:6-7,9).

We know Joshua paid attention, not only because of his success but also because after he gave orders to his military officers, they repeated the campaign theme back to him. "Only be strong and courageous!" (Joshua 1:18).

Shortly before King David passed away, he gave his son Solomon leadership advice he would need as Israel's next ruler. "Be strong and courageous, and do the work," David told him. "Do not be afraid or discouraged, for the LORD God, my God, is with you. He will not fail you or forsake you" (1 Chronicles 28:20).

Paul gave similar encouragement to persecuted believers in the early church: "Stand firm in the faith; be courageous; be strong" (1 Corinthians 16:13).

Many men and women today exhibit strong, courageous leadership in times of transition and peril. While their likenesses won't be carved on Mount Rushmore, memorials of a better kind will live in the hearts of the people they teach, the neighbors they help, the patients they treat, the victims they rescue, and the congregations they minister to.

So whenever we face difficult times, let's remember the rock-solid strength and courage many of our leaders exhibit—whether or not playwrights think they look the part.

Father God, let my service to you and to others be worth remembering, with or without an actual memorial. Amen.

10

Matching the Chip

GOD is sheer mercy and grace;
not easily angered, he's rich in love.

PSALM 103:8 MSG

When a homeowner hired a man to paint her living room, she handed the painter a little color chip and said, "I want the walls this same shade."

He mixed paint and covered one wall with it, but she wasn't satisfied. "It's not a perfect match," she explained.

He tried again. And again. Even after his fifth attempt, the woman continued to point to the chip. "You don't have quite the same color."

When he told a friend about it the following week, the friend asked, "Were you ever able to get the correct shade?"

"No. But she was okay after a long phone call to her mom."

"You mean her mother convinced her that a perfect match wasn't possible?"

"No," said the painter. "While she was on the phone, I painted the chip."

Often we perfectionists resort to "painting the chip" in order to present a flawless image to others. Perfection isn't possible, but we learned early in life that the only nice thing about being imperfect is the joy it brings to others. One of my most vivid lessons on that subject took place when a Sunday school teacher assigned me a "piece" to memorize for our holiday program.

Mom combed tangles from my never-cut locks. Then she washed

my hair and rolled it up in little blue rubber curlers to dry over the next two days. She did that only twice a year—at Easter and Christmas. When the curlers came out on Sunday morning, I put on my best dress, and we left for church in the family Studebaker.

Not everyone in my class was so prim and proper. Fidgety Willard Jackson always seemed to be getting into one scrape after another. Even his first and last names were troublesome. They both sounded like surnames to me, and I had trouble remembering their proper order.

My strict upbringing had already taught me that if I followed rules, I had a better chance of escaping punishment. So when the teacher stressed that we needed to deliver our pieces s-l-o-w-l-y, I paid attention.

The morning of the program, we all filed onto the platform. I proudly and loudly recited my holiday rhyme in a slow, measured cadence. My parents' beaming faces assured me I had done a good job.

Then it was my high-strung classmate's turn. He rattled off his piece so fast, it was unintelligible. To my surprise, the teacher didn't correct the boy, so I turned toward the end of the line and said loudly enough for him to hear, "Slow down, Jackson!"

The audience erupted in laughter.

I wanted to die. *Everyone's laughing at me for getting his first and last names mixed up!* I thought. I could only hope my gaffe would soon be forgotten. Instead, it became a Family Legend. I was in my fifties before I could even smile about it.

Many perfectionists who struggle with insecurity have been fettered by rigid rules and hammered by such Bible verses as Matthew 5:48, "Be perfect, therefore, as your heavenly Father is perfect."

Talk about an impossible goal! Some Bible scholars believe Jesus was saying that *aiming* for perfection is what's important, even if we can never truly be perfect. Others, looking at the scriptural context, assert that the previous verses in Matthew 5 emphasize a Christian's duty to love, so anyone who loves can be considered perfect. As a child, I knew nothing of those interpretations. All I knew was that in order to be acceptable, I couldn't make mistakes.

Most perfectionistic Christians have difficulty understanding the true nature of God. We were taught to be on constant guard because the Almighty's wrath was just a lightning bolt away.

Although I wasn't worried that my comment to antsy Willard would make me miss heaven, I *was* humiliated by what I perceived to be everyone's scorn and derision. I was ashamed because I'd failed to pull off a flawless performance. It took studying Scripture using correct principles of interpretation to see how loving, patient, and kind God really is. In fact, God knows better than we do that attaining perfection is impossible in this life. King David declared, "The Lord has compassion on those who fear him; for he knows how we are formed, he remembers that we are dust" (Psalm 103:13-14).

While it's never fun to let others see our dusty side, we struggling perfectionists need to realize we're valuable individuals even when we miss the mark. The good news is, God doesn't punish us for our fallibility. Instead, he makes up the difference when we trust in him. He also knows we don't need reminders of every commandment and regulation. We've already got 'em memorized. What we need is grace.

Coming to understand the true definition of grace stops me from panicking whenever I end up a slightly different shade than the model paint chip. I've learned the Master Painter will still make room for me in his palette.

Right there next to Jackson.

> Compassionate Father, thank you for releasing me
> from the prison of persnicketiness and for assuring
> me that you won't reject me when I fail to measure
> up to impossible standards of perfection. Amen.

11

The Taunted Shrub

*I am the vine; you are the branches. If you remain
in me and I in you, you will bear much fruit.*

JOHN 15:5

When a woman noticed her rosebush was covered with tiny insects, she carefully sprayed every stem and leaf. The next day the bugs were dead, but instead of falling off, they all seemed to be anchored firmly in place. That's when the woman realized she'd inadvertently used hair spray.

Plants can be in danger for all sorts of reasons. One spring, I discovered that after suffering through one of the nastiest winters on record, my prized topiary azalea had given up its flowery ghost. I grieved the loss. It had been a gift from a special friend. Although the spindly brown twigs added nothing to my yard's décor, I couldn't bring myself to yank them out of the ground. So I weeded and raked the rest of the flower bed and left the naked bush alone.

In a few weeks, colorful perennials pushed through the mulch, taunting the barren plant from every direction. Finally deciding to put the azalea out of its misery, I closed my gloved hand around the slender trunk to give it a tug. At the last second, I noticed tiny green shoots under my fingers. The plant was alive! By leaving it in the ground, I'd unwittingly given the azalea a chance to reveal the life it still contained.

For a long time after my son died of liver cancer on his first birthday, I couldn't pray or read the Bible. God had said no to the most desperate prayer I'd ever prayed, so what was the point in asking for anything else? Running across Bible accounts of people being healed or raised from the dead was simply too painful for me, so I set Scripture aside for a while. Why had God not also performed a miracle for my son?

Yet as wounded as I was, I didn't turn my back on God himself. Peter's words became mine: "Lord, to whom shall we go? You have the words of eternal life" (John 6:68). Gradually, I healed to the point where I was able to pray and study Scripture again and resume a growing relationship with my Savior. It took time. God gave me that time.

The prophet Isaiah compares God to a patient gardener—as well as a benevolent lamplighter—in describing his compassionate nature: "A bruised reed he will not break, and a smoldering wick he will not snuff out" (Isaiah 42:3).

I'm glad God understands when life's hard frosts have damaged our branches or burrowing rodents have injured our roots. Instead of relegating us to the compost heap, our loving Lord props us up and nourishes us so we can grow once again.

That's a comforting thought, whether our stems are drooping to the ground or merely shellacked with tiny bugs.

Lord, thank you for your patience and tender
care when I am too wounded to bloom. Help
me extend that grace to others. Amen.

The Sweet Smell of Spring

It is...an aroma pleasing to the LORD.

LEVITICUS 1:9

To add a romantic touch, one woman used lavender-scented laundry detergent when she washed the bedsheets and pillowcases. When her husband laid his head on the pillow that night, he sniffed. "What's this?"

"Guess," she said with a smile.

"I don't have any idea," he admitted. "But it smells like the stuff you put at the bottom of the hamster's cage."

After enduring many long winter nights, most of us are more than ready for the sweet aromas of spring. In Indiana, however, some consider the true heralds of spring to be skunks. One farmer in Elkhart County claims you can always tell when frost comes out of the ground because that's when skunks emerge. Spring is in the air...and it doesn't smell good.

For Elkhart County Highway Department employees, the emerging animals also mean more work. Almost daily during spring and summer, workers receive calls to remove the remains of skunks whose spray failed to intimidate oncoming cars. After encountering the critters when they're still alive, workers sometimes need to bathe in tomato juice to rid themselves of the persistent smell.

Odors matter to us. But did you know odors also matter to God? After the worldwide flood, Noah offered burnt sacrifices to the Lord. Then...

The LORD smelled the pleasing aroma and said in his heart: "Never again will I curse the ground because of humans, even though every inclination of the human heart is evil from childhood. And never again will I destroy all living creatures, as I have done" (Genesis 8:21).

As important as the aroma of that burnt sacrifice was to God, he later explained what was even more important: "I desire mercy, not sacrifice, and acknowledgment of God rather than burnt offerings" (Hosea 6:6).

Anyone who has been injured by life's hard knocks can take comfort in knowing how much God values mercy. He sees what we've been through. He cares when we've been wounded. It is his desire that others show us mercy, just as he himself is doing. Of course, we're to do the same. The sweetest aroma we can ever send back up to God is the mercy we show to those around us.

And nobody will ever confuse that smell with the stuff that lines hamster cages.

Heavenly Father, thank you for your mercy
and for reminding me how much it pleases you
when I am merciful toward others. Amen.

13

Dealing with Dual Citizenship

I know I'm only an outsider here among you.

Genesis 23:4 msg

Although our rural church was located some 75 miles north of Seattle, Ed still thought of us all as Seattle suburbanites.

"What does he know? He's from California," an old-timer grumbled good-naturedly.

One spring Ed joined our Sunday school class on an 80-mile trip north to Vancouver, BC. When we arrived at Stanley Park, the sun was peeping from behind gray clouds, but soon the skies darkened and rain sprinkles began. Ed turned up his coat collar. "I still can't get used to this blasted Seattle weather."

"*Seattle* weather!" exclaimed a friend. "We're not even in the same country. This is Canada!"

I know Americans who assume everyone born in English-speaking countries must think alike. One couple discovered differently on their trip north of the US border. The weather was so cold they stopped at a department store to purchase long underwear. When they asked a saleswoman where they could find what they were looking for, she directed them to the lingerie department.

"You know you're in Canada," the man muttered to his wife, "when long johns are considered lingerie."

As a nation, we often poke fun at our own regional differences. In 1945, one year after Warren G. Magnuson relocated from Washington State to Washington, DC, to begin his senatorial duties, he joked about his new hometown's "Northern charm and Southern efficiency."

Understanding differences can also help us maintain a proper perspective concerning our spiritual journey. While our ancestry and DNA come from this planet, God bestowed us with heavenly citizenship the moment we put our trust in Jesus Christ. Keeping that status in mind enables us to conquer all sorts of difficult circumstances, just as it helped the biblical heroes commended in Hebrews 11 for their remarkable walk of faith.

> How did they do it? They saw it way off in the distance, waved their greeting, and accepted the fact that they were transients in this world. People who live this way make it plain that they are looking for their true home. If they were homesick for the old country, they could have gone back any time they wanted. But they were after a far better country than that—heaven country. You can see why God is so proud of them, and has a City waiting for them (Hebrews 11:13-16 MSG).

Possessing this kind of dual citizenship is almost like arriving in a new country without ever leaving home, as Dorothy did in the *Wizard of Oz* when a twister deposited her house in a new land. Just a few steps from her own front door, she said, "Toto, I've a feeling we're not in Kansas anymore." Adjusting her thinking enabled Dorothy to handle new challenges.

A true understanding of our new nature and destination is what gives us the strength to "turn our backs on a godless, indulgent life, and…take on a God-filled, God-honoring life" (Titus 2:12 MSG). Stringent rules laid on us by domineering authorities, critical bosses, or pharisaical spiritual leaders do the opposite. They hinder and harm us.

God totally understands our desire to be free from abuse. We must understand that running from him never takes us in the right direction. He's the one who wants to rescue us and heal us from the damage we've suffered.

We may still have to endure cold or stormy weather from time to time, but let's remember we're not citizens of Kansas anymore. Or Seattle. Or the Land of Abuse. Our true home is the City that God has waiting for us. And there, we'll never need to ask where we can find long underwear.

Lord, I'm grateful you've made me a citizen of heaven. Help me complete the rest of my earthly journey in a way that honors you. Amen.

14

From the Ridiculous to the Sublime

Let us rejoice and be glad and give him glory!

REVELATION 19:7

It makes sense that a month beginning with a day of foolishness would also feature a slew of other offbeat commemorations. For instance, did you know April 2 is National Peanut Butter and Jelly Day, and April 17 is National Cheeseball Day? I'm not...fooling.

April also features National Garlic Day and Hug a Newsman Day—an interesting combination, to say the least. No wonder April is National Humor Month. Perhaps the lighthearted touch helps offset one of the year's gloomiest dates—April 15, Income Tax Day. Because Easter is usually one of April's special days too, the month contains holidays that truly range from the ridiculous to the sublime.

The sublime Resurrection Sunday is a wonderful time to celebrate our spiritual freedom. Christ's power over death not only means we have forgiveness of sin but also proves Jesus was who he claimed to be. John 2:22 tells us that after Christ "was raised from the dead, his disciples recalled what he had said. Then they believed the scripture and the words that Jesus had spoken."

If those who traveled with Jesus for three and a half years needed the power of the resurrection to be convinced fully of the gospel message, how much more do we need that power in our lives today? That's especially true for those who have been wounded on life's journey.

Maybe the folks who think up special calendar days are on to something. Our appreciation increases for anything we memorialize.

Let's meditate on that truth, whether we're hugging newsmen or noshing on garlic…or celebrating Christ's power over death, hell, and the grave—just as Christians have joyfully done for nearly 2000 years.

Lord Jesus, I gratefully celebrate your resurrection and the spiritual freedom it brings, along with the gift of laughter to brighten days often dampened by April showers. Amen.

PART TWO
Living Miraculously

A hospital patient was ecstatic. "You say my recovery is miraculous?" the woman squealed to her doctor. "Great! I was afraid I'd have to pay you."

Expecting miracles involves believing that God not only has the power but also the desire to work the miraculous in our lives. Whether it's receiving forgiveness for our sins, returning to health, being endowed with strength to live victoriously, or experiencing rescue from difficult situations, the first step is mustering faith to trust that God will hear and answer our prayers.

Sometimes we need miracles in our relationships, where we can do our part by honing the skill of gracious interaction with office assistants, neighbors, teachers, family members, and even ourselves. At other times, we need a supernatural touch to be set free from harmful patterns and behaviors that have bound us.

Whatever we lack, God stands ready to show us how to celebrate our victories instead of leaving us to wallow in our defeats. He kindly yet thoroughly cleanses us of old habits and prejudices so our inner wounds can heal and we can help those around us receive healing too.

The good news is that even when the whole world seems to be shaking, we don't have to rely solely on human expertise for protection and recovery. God is well able to do the miraculous whenever we're in need.

15

Expecting Miracles

*In his great mercy he has given us new birth
into a living hope through the resurrection
of Jesus Christ from the dead.*

1 PETER 1:3

Although he knew he had little chance of success, Ross tried to get his children to partake of Easter dinner after they'd already consumed a basketful of candy eggs and chocolate bunnies.

"They aren't going to eat," the children's grandmother told him. "This is Easter Sunday. What do you expect, a miracle?"

One of the joys of the Christian life is experiencing divine miracles. God's amazing power was never more evident than when Jesus rose from the dead.

Let's get one thing straight. Christ's crucified body was as dead as the tomb it lay in. Jesus wasn't in a coma or faking death—wild rationalizations some people come up with to deny the truth. Plenty of credible eyewitnesses confirmed the fact that his heart had stopped beating before he was wrapped in grave clothes and buried. As the apostle Peter declared some six weeks later, "God has raised this Jesus to life, and we are all witnesses of it" (Acts 2:32).

Divine miracles have continued since then—supernatural healing, protection, provision, and deliverance—in answer to Christians' faith-filled prayers. However, not every prayer is answered by a miracle. Sometimes God accompanies us *through* our trials instead of delivering us *out of* them. Unfortunately, feeling as if God is ignoring our pleas can lead to doubting that God loves us as much as Scripture claims he does.

That's understandable. And platitudes offered by well-meaning people—we have sin in our lives, we don't have enough faith, or God sent the trial to straighten us out—hurt more than they help. I know people who simply give up asking God for anything. Some even leave the Christian faith altogether.

After my son died, I stopped praying for a while. Wounded spiritually and emotionally, I wondered what the point was in asking God for anything when he'd denied the request that mattered to me the most. I would have given everything I owned in exchange for my son's life. *Evidently my faith wasn't enough*, I thought.

Although I couldn't pray in the traditional sense, I did beg God not to send along any further trial that would completely wipe out my remaining fragment of fragile faith. He answered. For a long time I was left undisturbed in an emotional fetal position. When I eventually gathered enough courage to formulate a request for something small, the reply came swiftly. I ventured another tiny request. The answer arrived before I'd even finished praying. Thus began my long road to spiritual recovery. As I reestablished my prayer life, I rediscovered the truth that in order to receive, one must ask (see James 4:2).

My recovery was not due to my own strength. As the apostle Paul shows, true power for victorious living comes from God's Spirit, who dwells within us.

> If the Spirit of him who raised Jesus from the dead is living in you, he who raised Christ from the dead will also give life to your mortal bodies because of his Spirit who lives in you (Romans 8:11).

I can only imagine the surge of power that rejuvenated Christ's corpse in that stone-cold tomb on Easter morning. Talk about a miracle! And yet Scripture declares that when God transformed us into new creations in Christ, the same Holy Spirit who brought Jesus back from the dead also took up residence in each one of us, imparting his vibrant, pulsating life to our mortal bodies.

I'm not claiming we have weird powers or that our physical bodies will never die. I don't fully understand how it all works. But I *have* seen enough miracles in my own life and in the lives of people around me to be convinced of the truth of Romans 8:11.

So every time we celebrate Christ's miraculous, glorious resurrection, let's remember we can anticipate miracles year-round—even on days that seem more ridiculous than sublime—because of the Mighty One who lives within us.

Thank you, Lord, for blessing my life with the power of the resurrection when I trust you as Savior. Help me to believe you for miracles all year long. Amen.

16

A Big Eraser on Tax Day

Have mercy on me, O God,
according to your unfailing love;
according to your great compassion
blot out my transgressions.

PSALM 51:1

When an airplane passenger learned his seatmate was a member of Congress, he asked, "Where are you from?"

"Washington," the congressman replied.

"Which one?" asked the first man. "Tax-*eating* Washington or tax-*paying* Washington?"

As a fifth-generation resident of tax-*paying* Washington, I join many fellow Americans in dreading April 15, the deadline for filing federal income-tax forms. That's why I was delighted to learn Rubber Eraser Day also occurs on April 15, the date in 1770 when Joseph Priestley discovered that a bit of rubber would remove pencil marks from paper. What a remarkable coincidence! The discovery of a substance capable of removing written mistakes shares a day with a deadline a lot of people wish they could erase from their lives.

Taxes aren't the only thing most of us would like to see blotted out. Certain liabilities in our memory banks may also tax us. However, we don't need to be dogged forever by past mistakes. God offers us something better than a big rubber eraser. When we repent and turn to God, he not only wipes out our sins but also sends us times of refreshing (see Acts 3:19).

- "Surely then you will…not keep track of my sin. My

offenses will be sealed up in a bag; you will cover over my sin" (Job 14:16-17).

- "You will again have compassion on us; you will tread our sins underfoot and hurl all our iniquities into the depths of the sea" (Micah 7:19).

If you have already repented of your transgressions, you can be confident God has heard you and has taken care of your payment obligation. Your sins are no longer listed on any celestial report form. On the cross, Christ erased them from your account. While you may still need to make restitution to those you've hurt, or you must endure certain consequences of past decisions, the "Amount you owe God" line reads zero, and you no longer have any reason to fear a future Audit Day.

So, on a day that might seem...*taxing*, let's rejoice in what our loving, generous God has done for us, no matter where on the tax-eating/tax-paying map we may reside.

Gracious heavenly Father, thank you for establishing a spiritual Rubber Eraser Day I can celebrate for the rest of my life. I am deeply grateful for your mercy. Amen.

17

Affirming Our Able Assistants

*Give to everyone what you owe them...if
respect, then respect; if honor, then honor.*

ROMANS 13:7

After cleaning out his office, a business owner put an old filing
cabinet on the sidewalk and taped a sign to it that read "Free."
Two days later, the cabinet was still there.

"I want that ugly thing gone!" he grumbled.

"Leave it to me," his assistant told him. She changed the sign to read,
"For Sale. $20." Within the hour, someone had stolen the cabinet.

That assistant deserved credit for her creative solution. Let's hope
she got it. Workers can become discouraged when their contributions are overlooked. Feeling like an underappreciated cog in corporate machinery has caused more than one faithful aide to resign.
In reality, the business world could not function without support
professionals.

Each year on Administrative Professionals Day, we have opportunity to remind those who perform secretarial, administrative-assistant, and receptionist work how much we appreciate them.
Although they usually don't get much recognition, they're the wind
beneath the wings of many folks who soar to prominence.

Take the apostle Paul, for instance, a notable church figure whose
correspondence became a major part of the New Testament. Did
you know he didn't pen those letters himself? Secretaries took dictation while Paul spoke. We're even told the name of one of those
secretaries—Tertius (see Romans 16:22).

Today, good assistants not only transcribe dictation but also answer phones, schedule appointments, send e-mails and text messages, manage databases, compose social-media updates, and do a thousand and one other vital tasks.

It's normal to get tired of behind-the-scenes work. Anyone can succumb to weariness and become bitter and burned out. I'm glad God understands how discouragement can sap one's energy and motivation. The Holy Spirit inspired Paul to offer this encouragement:

> Let us not become weary in doing good, for at the proper time we will reap a harvest if we do not give up. Therefore, as we have opportunity, let us do good to all people, especially to those who belong to the family of believers (Galatians 6:9-10).

We are to do good to all people, especially to those in the family of believers, even when they don't treat us well. Even when their weaknesses cause us pain and disappointment. Maybe we've become accustomed to business owners or managers who fail to express appreciation for our assistance, but surely leaders in faith communities are different, right? Not necessarily. The good thing is, if we focus on our service to God and not on the thoughtlessness of people around us, we can be confident of reaping an abundant harvest from the good deeds we sow.

And while we wait for those good works to sprout, let's honor everyone who performs vital services for us, including those who help dispose of ugly office equipment.

We appreciate you.

Lord, encourage all weary workers, bless them
abundantly, and reward them, I pray, for
their dedication and faithfulness. Amen.

18

Shouting *Olé* in the Family of God

*But God has put the body together...so that there
should be no division in the body...Now you are the
body of Christ, and each one of you is a part of it.*

1 CORINTHIANS 12:24-25,27

A tourist thought the Mexican restaurant looked like a great choice, but it wasn't open, so he decided to copy the name from a sign on the door and return another day. At that moment, a woman emerged from the restaurant and looked at him quizzically. The man explained what he was doing.

She glanced at what he'd jotted down. "That's not the restaurant's name," she said. Then she pointed to a sign above the awning. "This is the name. What you've written is Spanish for 'Closed on Mondays.'"

One of America's strengths, our ethnic diversity, is readily apparent on May 5, or as our Hispanic neighbors call it, Cinco de Mayo. The holiday is not Mexico's Independence Day, as many Americans think. This minor celebration commemorates Mexico's victory against French army invaders in the 1862 Battle of Puebla.

Although Cinco de Mayo is not a major holiday south of the border, in the past few years it *has* become a rousing fiesta in this country. I suspect restaurants may promote it in order to sell more tacos and enchiladas. But whatever the reason, celebrating one's heritage is an important part of being a citizen in a nation where most residents are descendants of immigrants.

Unfortunately, some descendants experience ill treatment because of their particular ethnic heritage or skin color. This is a grave transgression, not only against those on the receiving end of prejudice but also against our God, who created and deeply values every person on the planet.

Racial prejudice has been around for centuries. In Bible times, people who could trace their lineage to the patriarch Jacob clashed with other ethnic groups, both in wartime conflict and in religious disagreements. Then Jesus entered the equation and erased division lines between human beings. The apostle Paul explained it this way:

> The Messiah has made things up between us so that we're now together on this, both non-Jewish outsiders and Jewish insiders. He tore down the wall we used to keep each other at a distance…Then he started over. Instead of continuing with two groups of people separated by centuries of animosity and suspicion, he created a new kind of human being, a fresh start for everybody.
>
> Christ brought us together through his death on the Cross. The Cross got us to embrace, and that was the end of the hostility. Christ came and preached peace to you outsiders and peace to us insiders. He treated us as equals, and so made us equals (Ephesians 2:14-18 MSG).

Because Jesus Christ brought unity where strife and division had previously reigned, God's household is full of interesting, diverse, and colorful individuals—each of whom has been uniquely created by God.

So in an atmosphere of swinging piñatas, sizzling fajitas, and serenading mariachi bands, let's shout *olé* in thanks to God for including us in his wide, wonderful family.

That's a spiritual heritage worth celebrating even on Mondays.

Thank you, heavenly Father, for uniting your
children here on earth. Today I celebrate all of my
brothers and sisters in Christ, no matter where
they're from or what language they speak. Amen.

19

Thanking and Forgiving Our Teachers

So Christ himself gave...teachers.

EPHESIANS 4:11

Elementary students marched behind their teacher until she stopped at an intersection crosswalk. Asking, "Okay, children, why is it important for all of us to stay on the sidewalk?" she expected to hear something about traffic dangers.

Instead, one little voice piped up, "Because if we don't, we won't be covered by our health insurance!"

The youngster thought she'd learned something, but she needed guidance in her education. That's why we have instructors. Jesus referred to the importance of educators when he told his disciples, "The student who is fully trained will become like the teacher" (Luke 6:40 NLT). As followers of the ultimate Teacher, our goal is to become like Christ. But we also become a little bit like every other teacher we've ever learned from—both the good and not so good.

I know many people who struggle because they didn't receive adequate training when they were young. That neglect and/or misinformation had a lot to do with why they made poor choices in life and ended up on wrong paths.

I've spent a lifetime correcting errors I learned in my childhood. Through God's help—and after a thorough study of Scripture—I've overcome early prejudices instilled in me. I now realize that certain cultural practices labeled as sinful by my religious trainers are not banned by God after all. I've also discovered that some of my habits and concepts never should have been part of my upbringing. So

I'm faced with the need to forgive those who mishandled my training. I must also choose not to rehearse any "if only" regrets concerning erroneous lessons that sent me on time-wasting detours. I'm sure all those who taught me truly meant well. Their desire was to help me become a godly person, not to ruin my life.

Unfortunately, that's not the case for everyone. Some people have been deeply hurt by authority figures with evil intentions. Those who begin the journey toward forgiveness find that healing and restoration can grow to fill spaces where anger and the desire for revenge used to smolder. Forgiveness doesn't imply approval of what happened. It unlocks the door so the wounded person can escape from a spiritual and emotional prison.

Being a teacher is a solemn responsibility. The apostle James cautioned, "Not many of you should become teachers, my fellow believers, because you know that we who teach will be judged more strictly" (James 3:1). James isn't saying we should avoid teaching altogether. We *should* grow to the point of being able to educate others instead of always being students ourselves (see Hebrews 5:12). But it's important to remember we change lives by what we teach and model—for good *or* for bad.

So let's honor instructors who helped us remain on life's sidewalk of safety. And let's forgive those whose input shoved us into dangerous traffic, whether or not that was their intention. Even long after we have left inadequate classrooms, our loving, all-powerful Teacher is able to transform faulty lessons into godly wisdom we can pass along to fellow pedestrians at life's crosswalks.

> *Lord, thank you for wise teachers in my life. Help me to*
> *let go of any resentment toward unwise teachers, and*
> *bring good out of negative situations in my life that have*
> *resulted from poor instruction. I also ask that you keep*
> *me from repeating those mistakes with others. Amen.*

20

The Ancient Art of Motherly Nagging

King Solomon...got up and welcomed her,
bowing respectfully, and returned to his
throne. Then he had a throne put in place for
his mother, and she sat at his right hand.

1 KINGS 2:19 MSG

S cottish comedian Billy Connolly defines an intellectual as someone who can listen to the *William Tell* Overture without thinking of the Lone Ranger.

I don't know whether comedienne Anita Renfroe thinks of the
ancient archer or the masked horseman when she sings that mel-
ody, but a video of her performance has gone viral and has received
millions of hits.

During the three-minute song, Anita rattles off everything a
mom says to her kids in a 24-hour period—phrases such as brush
your teeth, eat your breakfast, wash behind your ears, clean your
room, were you born in a barn, close your mouth when you chew,
I'll count to three, I don't care who started it, and look at me when
I'm talking. Especially clever is the triplet, "Get a job, get a life, get
a PhD."

Just one day of the year isn't often enough to convey sufficient
gratitude for our mothers' valuable input. Perhaps that's one reason
God commands us in Exodus 20:12 to honor our mothers—along
with our fathers—continually, "so that you may live long in the land
the LORD your God is giving you."

Did you recognize any of Anita's lines? Motherly instruction isn't all that new. Some 3000 years ago the wisest man on earth urged his son, "Do not forsake your mother's teaching" (King Solomon in Proverbs 6:20). Maybe the young man's mother was like Anita and continually reminded her son to close the tent flap, straighten his headpiece, and finish his bowl of camel stew. Who knows?

Proverbs 31 lists some of a godly mother's attributes:

> She is worth far more than rubies...
> She speaks with wisdom,
>   and faithful instruction is on her tongue...
> Her children arise and call her blessed;
>   her husband also, and he praises her:
> "Many women do noble things,
>   but you surpass them all."
> Charm is deceptive, and beauty is fleeting;
>   but a woman who fears the LORD is to be praised.
> Honor her for all that her hands have done,
>   and let her works bring her praise at the city gate
>   (Proverbs 31:10,26,28-30).

Children whose mothers are like this sterling example usually don't need much prodding to express their love and appreciation. But not everyone is so blessed. Some people grew up feeling unheard, disrespected, and misunderstood. They've been deeply wounded by arrows of complaints, criticism, and put-downs.

As Proverbs 18:21 points out, "The tongue has the power of life and death." Death from a mother's tongue usually creates anger and bitterness. If her offspring were to choose a verse to represent their feelings, it might be Judges 16:16: "With such nagging she prodded him day after day until he was sick to death of it."

Yet the command to honor mothers still stands. One key to fulfilling that commandment is to honor the position even when we can't respect the way someone treats us. It also helps to consider the motivation behind the nagging. Most mothers offer advice because they want the best for their children. Sometimes they regret their own parenting mistakes and attempt to compensate with ramped-up suggestions, clinging to the hope that one day they'll get it right. Every mother on the planet has her own struggles.

God understands how difficult it can be to forgive years of verbal abuse. It can also be hard when mothers continue to nag grown children about their hairstyles, careers, living arrangements, significant others, and grandchildren—or the lack thereof.

That may be why the Holy Spirit inspired Paul to remind us that the instruction to honor parents "is the first commandment with a promise" (Ephesians 6:2). A reward provides extra motivation to forgive critical, unsupportive people.

Keep in mind that honoring someone doesn't mean allowing more damage. It is possible to show honor by overlooking some slights while refusing—with respect—to accept others. It also involves asking God to bless those who hurt us. If at first you can't think of anything specific to say, simply ask the Lord to do in your mother's life whatever he desires to do, trusting that our loving God will never answer that prayer in a way that would cause you additional pain.

Whether motherly nagging has helped you, hurt you, or simply annoyed you, choosing to show honor out of obedience to God will open channels of healing in your life. Learning how to break the cycle of destructive nagging is also a wonderful gift to give our own children. So if you're a parent doing the best job you can, take joy in knowing that giving godly instruction to your sons and daughters will bless them all their lives.

And who knows? A video of your wisdom might even go viral on the Internet.

> Lord, thank you for the godly training I have received.
> I appreciate your promise of long life as a reward for
> choosing to honor my parents. Help me to forgive any
> less-than-perfect moments that occurred. I know my
> parents did their best, just as I am trying to do. Amen.

21

Mountains That Shake— and Other Calamities

"Though the mountains be shaken
and the hills be removed,
yet my unfailing love for you will not be shaken
nor my covenant of peace be removed,"
says the LORD, who has compassion on you.

ISAIAH 54:10

When a real-estate agent told a couple he could show them a listing with a tremendous view, they seemed eager to look at it. Once inside the home, the agent swept back living-room drapes with a flourish to reveal majestic scenery framed by a large picture window. He waited for gasps of delight.

Instead, the puzzled husband said, "Where's the view? Those mountains must be blocking it."

When mountains block us from something we desire, we often assume the situation will never change. After all, aren't mountains immovable? Not necessarily. More than three decades ago, a huge part of Mount Saint Helens in Washington State rose straight into the atmosphere while another gigantic section liquefied and flowed into valleys below.

I lived some 175 miles away from the mountain and was getting ready for church at 8:32 Sunday morning, May 18, 1980, when I heard a loud bang outside. I soon learned the volcano had erupted. Although the event had been predicted, what actually took place far exceeded anyone's expectations.

A magnitude 5.1 earthquake started an enormous avalanche on the mountain's north slope. A searing blast of volcanic gas, pumice, ash, and rock bits spurted horizontally from the mountain at 300 miles per hour. Within ten minutes an ash plume reached ten miles into the atmosphere.

Furnace-like winds reduced evergreen forests in the "blowdown zone" to graveyards of denuded trees, all lying in the same direction like quills on a porcupine. Fringing that area, hot gases and flying rock fragments killed trees—but left them standing—in a 42-square-mile "scorch zone."

Meanwhile, snow and ice, including several entire glaciers, melted into large lahars (volcanic mudslides), destroying bridges and homes as they surged downhill. Across the state, the noon sky turned midnight black. Ash fell like snow, eventually spreading over 11 states. The eruption continued for nine hours. Some folks thought the end of the world had come.

Fifty-seven people died in the eruption. Only four were in the restricted zone, and they had special permission to be there. Everyone was caught off guard.

Some people have experienced eruptions of volcanic proportion in their own lives. Perhaps they thought they would be safe, but they suffered unfathomable loss, pain, betrayal, abuse, financial ruin... Hope was blasted, security incinerated. Then, instead of receiving help and encouragement, some were targets of blame, accusation, gossip, and shunning.

If that describes your situation, take comfort in knowing you are not doomed to live forever in the valley of destruction. God sees where you are. He knows how difficult it can be for you to forgive those who hurt you—along with those who should have protected you or responded when you asked for help. In spite of what was done to you, you can leave justice in God's hands and ask to be rescued from the lifeless blast zone you wander in now.

Centuries ago the prophet Isaiah had a marvelous word for

discouraged inhabitants of Jerusalem who had suffered devastating loss:

> Yet the LORD longs to be gracious to you;
>   therefore he will rise up to show you compassion.
> For the LORD is a God of justice.
>   Blessed are all who wait for him! (Isaiah 30:18).

After the 1980 eruption, scientists surveyed the lunar-like landscape on Mount Saint Helens. They predicted it would take a very long time for vegetation and animal life to return to the bare rock and steaming, cracked mud left behind. However, within just a few years, the ground again teemed with insects, and innumerable gophers churned the soil. Trees and wildflowers dotted the pumice plain, fish swam in lakes, and birds built nests. Even a huge elk herd roamed the area once again.

Watching the shaken mountain recover reminds us we can also experience restoration, no matter how devastating our losses have been. The divine promise to us is, "You will weep no more. How gracious he will be when you cry for help! As soon as he hears, he will answer you" (Isaiah 30:19).

Let's not be afraid to cry out to our Lord, who promises to listen. And when the answer arrives, we'll find that destroyer mountains no longer block any of the majestic blessings God has lovingly prepared for us.

Merciful Father, thank you for your ongoing restoration of what has been damaged in my life—including my trust in you. How wonderful to know you desire to be gracious to me always. In times of devastation, help me to believe I'll see good days again when I dare to ask you for them. Amen.

22

Stripping Wire to Its Valuable Core

The glory that will be revealed in us...

Romans 8:18

For years, whenever an appliance died, I would snip off the cord and save it in case I needed to use it later when repairing another gadget. Then I realized that if I hadn't used the cords in 20 years, maybe it would be safe to get rid of them. The elevated price of copper also helped me come to that decision.

Recyclers pay more money for wire that's not wrapped with casing and insulation, so I got out wire strippers. The tool didn't work very well. An online source suggested softening casings in a candle flame. I didn't remember to use gloves when tugging on the "softened" plastic until a blister formed on my left index finger.

After a large bowl brimmed with curly bare-copper strands from old vacuum and lamp cords, I turned my attention to some industrial wire that had sat in the garage for 30 years. I made a small slit in the casing, grasped the edge of the plastic with a pair of pliers, and stripped long sections at a time. The process raised only a small blister on my right index finger.

During my quiet time the next morning, I realized that just as larger wire is easier to strip than tiny wire, so also I endure emotional "stripping" more easily after my soul has matured as the result of a spiritual growth spurt. Already-accomplished healing of inner wounds allows me to move more quickly through each new session of recognizing personal triggers, identifying original sources of wounding, and forgiving those who've hurt me.

When our core is no longer obscured, it's easier to see ourselves from God's point of view. Here's what Scripture says about our worth in God's sight:

- "Look at the birds of the air; they do not sow or reap or store away in barns, and yet your heavenly Father feeds them. Are you not much more valuable than they?" (Matthew 6:26).

- "So don't be afraid; you are worth more than many sparrows" (Matthew 10:31).

- "Consider the ravens: They do not sow or reap, they have no storeroom or barn; yet God feeds them. And how much more valuable you are than birds!" (Luke 12:24).

- "For the Lord God is a sun and shield;
    the Lord bestows favor and honor;
  no good thing does he withhold
    from those whose walk is blameless" (Psalm 84:11).

Stripping sessions are never fun, but it's a joy later to watch the reflection of God's favor shimmering off our bowls of curly copper worth. And that helps us to forget the discomfort of any blisters that may have formed in the process.

> *Thank you, heavenly Father, for stripping sessions*
> *that reveal my spirit's valuable core. Help me to*
> *understand the intrinsic worth you gave each one*
> *of us at creation. Help me also to curb my desire to*
> *remove other people's casings for them. I will leave*
> *that process in your capable hands. Amen.*

23

Yellow-Ribboned Reminders

I thank my God every time I remember you.

PHILIPPIANS 1:3

To honor a family member stationed overseas with the military, Margaret and her five-year-old granddaughter tied a yellow ribbon around a tree in Margaret's yard. "Grandmom, why are we doing this?" the girl asked.

"We're doing it for your cousin," Margaret replied.

As the youngster watched her grandmother straighten the bow, she said in a quiet voice, "A tree doesn't seem like much of a gift."

The actual gift, of course, was the remembrance—which is the whole point of patriotic holidays. Memorial Day, for instance, began after the Civil War as a way to honor Union soldiers who had died in battle. Then it expanded to commemorate all US military personnel who made the ultimate sacrifice in service to their country. By the early twentieth century, people used Memorial Day as a time to visit the graves of their deceased relatives whether or not they had served in the military. My twice-widowed mother follows that custom and leaves flowers at the tombstones of her late husbands, parents, in-laws, and infant grandson.

In the Old Testament, God instituted a number of memorials to celebrate victories, miracles of deliverance, and other marvelous events. Note that he didn't instruct the people to memorialize defeats.

Some of us possess an entire collection of thought-life memorials that serve as reminders of times when we were rejected, forgotten, abused, or cheated, or when we suffered some other kind of bad treatment. To move forward in our healing, we must smash those memorials and erect new ones that will remind us of God's patience, love, grace, kindness, mercy, and healing power. For instance, every time a prayer is answered, we can add it to our new memorial as a reminder of God's love and faithfulness.

The Lord knows we need memory joggers. Memorial Day and other patriotic holidays remind us to express gratitude for those who have fought to win or maintain our country's freedom. We can also let the holiday remind us of how our Lord died to purchase our spiritual freedom. There isn't enough yellow ribbon in the entire world to adequately memorialize that momentous event.

Thank you, Lord, for a special day to remember and
show gratitude for the blood that was spilled to
ensure my freedom. I am truly grateful. Amen.

24

Creaky Joints and Other Distractions

*We know that the whole creation has been groaning as
in the pains of childbirth right up to the present time.*

ROMANS 8:22

By the time we arrived at the high school grandstands, every seat had been taken, so my sister, my brother-in-law, and I stood behind ropes encircling the football field. That gave us a prime view of my petite niece in her gown and mortarboard as she and her classmates marched to the underclassman band's brave attempt at "Pomp and Circumstance."

I'd worn comfy shoes, so I didn't mind standing. But after the national anthem, the principal asked everyone near the ropes to sit down so we wouldn't block the view of those behind us. I wanted to flash my AARP card for an exemption. Instead, I bent creaky joints to sit with others on the damp grass for the 90-minute ceremony. When one leg went numb, I shifted my weight until the other leg started to tingle. My sister sacrificed her windbreaker so we wouldn't end up with embarrassing wet spots on our jeans, but the thin nylon couldn't protect our bones from the hard ground.

Have you ever noticed how difficult it is to pay attention when you're uncomfortable?

In his classic book *The Problem of Pain*, C.S. Lewis asserted that "God whispers to us in our pleasures, speaks in our conscience, but shouts in our pains: it is His megaphone to rouse a deaf world."[1] I've heard the famous quote often, especially in sermons.

Perhaps someone has said that line to you in difficult situations, but you weren't comforted by being called so deaf and dense that pain was the only way God could get your attention.

Although God sent Old Testament prophets to warn nations of coming judgment if they didn't repent, I do not find passages of Scripture in which God used a megaphone to rattle emotionally wounded people. I *can*, however, find plenty of promises of God's comfort and his mighty deliverance when we call upon him. That is not to say we'll live charmed lives. But often we don't receive supernatural help because we don't ask for it—or we're too impatient to wait until it arrives. If this describes your current situation, take heart. Better things lie ahead. In 2 Corinthians 5:5, Paul reminds us God "has given us the Spirit as a deposit, guaranteeing what is to come."

Just as my creaky joints felt better when I was able to get back on my feet on that football field, so too God revives me after I've been wounded emotionally. And he's never used pain's megaphone to do it.

Gracious God, send comfort and healing today to everyone
in mental, physical, spiritual, or emotional pain. Amen.

25

Wisdom for Overwhelmed Fathers

I will teach you wisdom's ways
and lead you in straight paths.
When you walk, you won't be held back;
when you run, you won't stumble.
Take hold of my instructions; don't let them go.
Guard them, for they are the key to life.

PROVERBS 4:11-13 NLT

When a six-year-old was leaving with his father to attend the movies for the first time, his mother warned him the film was known for being very sad. But the boy still wanted to go. When he returned, the mom asked her son if he had cried at any point.

"Yes," he said.

"Which part?" Mom asked.

"The part where Daddy wouldn't buy me any popcorn."

It's not easy being a dad. Fatherhood involves supporting, protecting, guiding, leading, and a whole gamut of other responsibilities for which many men aren't sure they're fully qualified, especially when their own fathers may not have been good role models.

God understands. That's one reason he inspired the apostle James to write, "If any of you lacks wisdom, you should ask God, who gives generously to all without finding fault, and it will be given to you" (James 1:5).

If there's anything that requires wisdom, it's parenting. But often we're so busy dealing with our own scars, we're not sure how to nurture impressionable young lives in our care. Sometimes, fathers not only are responsible for their own children but also care for stepchildren, grandchildren, and/or foster kids.

While being a good father has always been a challenge, today's social climate can make the task seem especially daunting. All too often, trauma has tragically scarred innocent lives at an early age, requiring those in parenting roles to possess even more insight.

Scripture does give fathers specific instruction not to exasperate their children (Ephesians 6:4) or embitter them (Colossians 3:21). But exactly *how* to rear children without making them bitter or exasperated requires wisdom. Divine wisdom. The kind God invites us all to ask him for.

> Trust GOD from the bottom of your heart;
>   don't try to figure out everything on your own.
> Listen for GOD's voice in everything you do,
>   everywhere you go;
>   he's the one who will keep you on track.
> Don't assume that you know it all.
>   Run to GOD! (Proverbs 3:5-7 MSG).

How wonderful it is to know you can trust God for assistance in whatever parenting challenges you may face. Even those involving theater concessions.

Loving heavenly Father, I need help in nurturing
those you've put in my care. Thank you for providing
wisdom in every situation I encounter. Amen.

26

Seeing Through Dirt

Nothing in all creation is hidden from God's sight.

HEBREWS 4:13

After five years of postgraduate work, Zachary finally realized his dream of becoming an archaeologist. A museum soon hired him to supervise an archaeological dig. One day while the crew labored in sweltering weather, a little boy and his mom stopped at the edge of the hole to observe all the activity.

After the mother watched Zachary, covered head to toe with mud and holding a pickax, she turned to her son. "See what will happen if you don't finish school?" she said. "You'll end up just like that man."

No matter what level of education one may have, digging in dirt is hard labor. I learned that a few years ago when I had to excavate a trench behind my house. The job sounded simple enough, but the minute I started to dig, I ran into problems.

Those problems included underground rocks and tree roots. I never knew that shoveling with a spade and prodding with a pickax could be so bone jarring. I thought, *If only I could see through dirt. Then I'd know how to avoid the obstacles. What I need is X-ray vision, like God's.*

God can see through anything. Scripture writers have chronicled God's ability to search our hearts and minds.

- *King David.* "You have searched me, LORD, and you know me" (Psalm 139:1).

- *The prophet Jeremiah.* "I the LORD search the heart and examine the mind" (Jeremiah 17:10).

- *The apostle Paul.* "He who searches our hearts knows the mind of the Spirit, because the Spirit intercedes for God's people in accordance with the will of God" (Romans 8:27).

- *John the Revelator.* "All the churches will know that I [the Son of God] am he who searches hearts and minds" (Revelation 2:23).

God has a crystal-clear view of everything about us—from our love for him to our impatience, from our desire to serve him to our fears and feelings of inadequacy. But he loves us and wants only the best for us, so he reveals buried treasures we never knew we possessed. He also offers to show us where rocks and roots lie hidden so we can ask him to remove them. None of us will ever totally complete our personal archeological digs, but as God helps us search through the soil of our lives, our response to what is revealed determines our destiny.

Solomon, a king divinely blessed with extraordinary wisdom, declared, "Whoever heeds life-giving correction will be at home among the wise" (Proverbs 15:31).

It's exhilarating to realize that paying attention to God's correction will put us in the same class as the wisest people on earth—even if we never finish school.

Dear Lord, help me to trust in you and in your ability to see every part of my life. Thank you for removing obstacles so I can grow in wisdom. Amen.

PART THREE
Participating Joyfully

Changing our understanding of how God interacts with us can transform the way we participate in life. We can drag through our days under the weight of fear, worry, and dread, or we can allow God to reveal to us his truth about our inestimable value.

Such revelation can give us wisdom when choosing our activities. Erma Bombeck illustrated that wisdom when she sent her now-famous RSVP to a pro-am ski tournament: "I do not participate in any sport with ambulances at the bottom of a hill."

Joyful participation comes from understanding that God always has our best interests at heart. We can safely trust God's map for our journey. Knowing that we're truly valuable in his sight helps us treat everyone else with that same value, and it also adds meaning to mundane tasks as we fulfill our divinely appointed destiny. Then even the jaws of distress are unable to keep us trapped, and we are liberated to travel through life with zest.

We might not be able to avoid life's dangers as easily as Erma avoided risks in sports, but we can be sure that we will never tumble down hills without finding spiritual ambulances at the bottom—staffed by the Great Physician himself.

27

The Joyfully Serious Business of Banner-Waving

Lift up a banner in the land!

JEREMIAH 51:27

A woman browsing at the jewelry counter of a posh department store asked to see American flag pins. The salesclerk showed her numerous models in a large variety of gold, silver, and enamel settings, either unadorned or encrusted with gems. None of the jewelry satisfied the customer. Finally, she asked, "Don't you have an American flag pin in another color combination?"

On patriotic holidays many Americans display red, white, and blue banners to show love and respect for their country. The psalmist David mentions banners of a different kind to show love and respect for God: "My arms wave like banners of praise to you" (Psalm 63:4 MSG).

Have you ever thought of your arms being like banners before the Lord? The metaphor is an apt one. Worshipful banner waving has hidden benefits. Praising God with exuberance opens us up to emotional and spiritual healing as well as an increased ability to enjoy life to the full. Psalm 20 talks about waving banners in celebration when God...

- answers when you're in distress,
- protects you,
- sends you help and support,

- remembers and accepts all your sacrifices, and
- gives you the desire of your heart.

The list is followed by this declaration: "May we shout for joy over your victory and lift up our banners in the name of our God" (verse 5).

When we wave banners and fly flags to express emotion, we also declare loyalty to the entity the flag represents. In the United States, patriotic holidays remind each American what a privilege it is to be a citizen of our country. When we wave banners of praise to our Lord—in whatever color combination we prefer—we celebrate the privilege of belonging to the kingdom of God.

What will your banner waving look like today?

Heavenly Father, I wave banners in gratitude for
your blessing and healing in my life. Amen.

28

As Diligent as Summer Ants

Lazy hands make for poverty,
but diligent hands bring wealth.

PROVERBS 10:4

When school let out for the summer, one teen became increasingly irresponsible about performing household chores. He wouldn't even get involved in training the family's new puppy.

His mom, an overwhelmed single parent with a full-time job, finally went to the library to borrow a book on dog training. While there, she also selected a book on the continuing challenge of rearing teenagers.

At the checkout counter, the librarian glanced at both titles and commented wryly, "The dog is going to be a lot easier."

While summer can mean family vacation trips, a chance to enjoy sunshine, and a break for school students, the daily grind continues for the most part. Summer solstice doesn't mean we can neglect our duties. Scripture tells us that God commends those who make hay while the sun shines. "He who gathers crops in summer is a prudent son, but he who sleeps during harvest is a disgraceful son" (Proverbs 10:5).

Another proverb supports this observation with an illustration from the animal kingdom. Proverbs 30 lists four creatures that are wise in spite of their small size. Verse 25 (MSG) says, "Ants—frail as they are, get plenty of food in for the winter."

To illustrate the importance of carrying out our tasks responsibly, Jesus told his disciples a parable about a businessman and his employees. Just before the man left on a journey, he entrusted each of his staff members with money to invest. Two of the employees put the capital to good use and increased their boss's wealth. When the businessman returned, he was pleased: "Good work! You did your job well. From now on be my partner" (Matthew 25:21,23 MSG).

A third employee didn't fare so well. He hoarded his allotted funds, gaining not even one cent. "The master was furious. 'That's a terrible way to live! It's criminal to live cautiously like that! If you knew I was after the best, why did you do less than the least?'" (Matthew 25:26 MSG).

It's not easy to delay gratification to take care of necessary tasks when we'd rather do something fun. However, life's winters always roll around, and people who've prepared for them are glad they were diligent during good times.

Being responsible in this area includes working on spiritual and emotional healing. Choosing to forgive others or even trusting God again can be hard work. But when we face difficult tasks head-on, we'll be glad we made the effort.

And our rewards will probably include more than having just a well-trained puppy in the house—or well-trained offspring, as the case may be.

Dear Lord, I pray for strength to be diligent in
everything you give me to do, including carrying out
tasks that help me recover from my hurts. Amen.

29

Changing the Picture

See what great love the Father has lavished on us.

Like most toddlers, my grandson loved to test barriers that barred him from tantalizing delights. When my daughter caught him sampling fresh mint leaves he'd swiped from her herb garden, she laughed. "You're sneaky!" she told him.

The word immediately became a new favorite. He ran around the house yelling, "Neek-nee! Neek-nee! Neek-nee!"

I'm thankful my daughter and son-in-law are great parents. They shower their son with attention, respect, and unconditional love. That doesn't mean my grandson will grow up unscathed, but it certainly increases his chances for emotional wholeness.

Many of us didn't have that kind of upbringing. Criticism, disapproval, and even abuse may have been the norm. Our collateral damage often includes a warped view of God.

Just when I think I've put away my early picture of God as a humorless enforcer, always watching for an opportunity to smash me with his cosmic billy club, that view pops up again. Sometimes I think my emotions are a bit like the dwarves' in C.S. Lewis's *The Last Battle*. Once their trust was broken by an Aslan imposter, they wouldn't risk trusting again, even when the genuine Aslan showed up.

I don't want to be like that. I want to allow God's Word to soak into my wounded spirit so I can fully trust "the God and Father of our Lord Jesus Christ, the Father of compassion and the God of all comfort" (2 Corinthians 1:3).

When my grandson was three, he had to undergo a serious dental procedure involving general anesthesia. Medical professionals took him from his parents into another room, and as the anesthesiologist brought a face mask close, my grandson screamed in fear.

"It's okay," the doctor said, assuring him he'd just go to sleep.

"No!" my grandson wailed. "I'm *not* going to sleep!" Of course, he succumbed quickly to the drugs, and the dental procedure went much better than expected, to everyone's great relief.

Throughout the entire ordeal, each decision his agonized parents made was for their beloved son's benefit. How like our relationship with God! What happens to us in life may cause us to be afraid of God, but in reality, our heavenly Father always has our best interests at heart.

Even when we've been sneaky.

Loving heavenly Father, let me see your true divine nature. In each new crisis I face, please heal my misconceptions so I can see you for the gracious, compassionate, forgiving God you really are. Amen.

30

Escaping the Jaws of Distress

*With us is the Lord our God to help
us and to fight our battles.*

2 Chronicles 32:8

A father thought his little boy, Will, might enjoy the pageantry and excitement of a Civil War battle reenactment. But booming cannons frightened the poor child nearly to death. During a lull, Will's dad was finally able to calm his son down.

Then a Confederate general shouted, "Fire at will!"

Recently, when it seemed life was shouting "Fire at Diana!" way too often, I came across a wonderful verse I hadn't noticed before in the book of Job. It says God "is wooing you from the jaws of distress to a spacious place free from restriction, to the comfort of your table laden with choice food" (Job 36:16).

I received it as a message from the heavenly Father to my fearful heart and scribbled the verse on a scrap of paper. Every time I saw those words taped next to my computer, I pondered the mystery of why people caught in the jaws of distress need to be wooed to escape. Isn't it normal to run from bondage at the first opportunity?

Whether it's normal or nuts, many people remain in misery's mouth even when nothing visible holds them there. That's because they're trapped by far more than mere jawbones.

Jonah is a good example of this phenomenon. The prophet's bondage began a long time before he disappeared inside that enormous fish many of us learned about in Sunday school. Cords of confinement had already coiled around Jonah by the time he received his unwanted commission to warn Ninevites of coming destruction.

Although I've known the Jonah account for decades, only in the past few years have I understood the real reason why Jonah rebelled against God's command. Nineveh was the capital of the Assyrian empire, a regime famous for cruelty. Excavated stone carvings depict many scenes of battles and impalements. One Assyrian king boasted about filling the streets of conquered Babylon with the corpses of the city's inhabitants, both young and old. Other accounts tell of the Assyrians piling heads of decapitated soldiers against city walls.

Those Assyrians were far more intimidating than an entire battlefield of Confederate generals. Like everyone else in the ancient Middle East, Jonah hoped God would pulverize them. Instead, the Lord commanded Jonah to give the citizens of Assyria's capital city a chance to get off scot-free.

Jonah's natural human desire for revenge acted like a powerful steroid on those jaws of distress, causing the metaphorical mandibles to grow even more threatening. When the prodigal prophet booked passage for Tarshish—a destination about as far away from Nineveh as he could get—those jaws imprisoned him more securely than a granite guardhouse.

Today, many Christians are bound by jaws of distress that grew from invisible scars of past hurts. When they begged God for justice, they may have heard only that they were simply to love their enemies and pray for those who persecuted them (see Matthew 5:44).

Choosing to love and pray for our enemies seems like a strange way to gain freedom. That's why we usually need wooing to do it. However, instead of being wooed with fragrant bouquets and boxes of chocolates, we're often flipped from the frying pan into the fire. Or, in Jonah's case, from a small ship's sea-tossed belly to a big fish's slime-lined stomach.

Can you imagine what it must have been like to slither down the fish's throat into that stinky, inky-black intestinal cavity? Jonah had never intended to become a sea creature's snack. Instead, he'd offered to die so his shipmates could live—and, perhaps, so he could end his own personal chaos. The crew resisted his offer at first and tried to row the battered ship back to land. But when the storm worsened, they threw Jonah overboard to appease God—and prayed that their action wouldn't be considered murder.

It was as if the storm had been Velcroed to the doomed man. As Jonah sank, the water's surface above him grew calm, but his own turmoil intensified. Once he was inside the monster fish, seaweed wrapped itself around his head and gastric juices corroded his skin. Instead of a quick end by drowning, it seemed he would be digested to death.

The word *wooing* doesn't come to mind when I think of those circumstances, but the desperate situation motivated Jonah to use the only remaining keys he had that would set him free. He called out to the Lord, repented of his disobedience, and accepted the obnoxious order. "What I have vowed I will make good," he promised. "I will say, 'Salvation comes from the LORD'" (Jonah 2:9).

Jonah's new attitude sliced through his invisible chains of hatred and unforgiveness. And once those chains were severed, God opened the fish's jaws, and the fish "vomited Jonah onto dry land" (Jonah 2:10).

To be sure, it was an unpleasant exit from an unpleasant environment so Jonah could embark on an unpleasant expedition. But God gave him success.

> The people of Nineveh believed God's message, and from the greatest to the least, they declared a fast and put on burlap to show their sorrow...
>
> When God saw what they had done and how they had put a stop to their evil ways, he changed his mind and did not carry out the destruction he had threatened (Jonah 3:5,10 NLT).

If I lived in a desert city hundreds of miles from the seacoast and a man with shriveled, acid-burned skin and a hunk of seaweed dangling from one ear warned me that in 40 days I'd be toast, I would repent too.

Did the people's repentance make Jonah happy? Not on your life. He still wanted to see the Assyrians pulverized. But in the last verse of the book, God reminded him of the city's 120,000 innocent citizens who deserved a chance to repent. (And many of us appreciate God's concern for all their animals.)

No matter what jaws of distress may be clamping down on you right now, rest assured God is wooing you to a spacious place free from restriction. All you need to do is respond.

Once you enter your unrestricted spaces, remember that even though cannons may still boom at you from time to time, no scary scenario will ever be a match for Almighty God—the same God who has promised to fight your battles when you rely on him.

Merciful Lord, I respond to your wooing to
escape the jaws of distress. Help me to trust you
during the process of deliverance. Amen.

31

Making Assumptions

Jesus knew what they were thinking.

LUKE 5:22

A few years ago, I received notice that my health insurance premium would go up 56 percent the following month.

I was just as healthy as ever. I didn't take prescription meds. My blood pressure and cholesterol levels were great. I slept well, exercised regularly, and maintained a healthy diet. I rarely even caught colds. So I appealed to the insurance rep on the phone. "Doesn't it help that I've never made a single claim with your company?"

"Unfortunately, no," she said. "Most of the increase is because you moved into a new age bracket on your last birthday."

Even though I was probably one of the healthiest AARP members you'd ever meet, the insurance firm made assumptions about my actuarial risk and charged me accordingly.

Sometimes assumptions within the insurance industry can lead to amusing situations, such as when management strongly urged all agents at one company to attend an informational meeting led by a speaker they had not heard before. Agents responding to management's "suggestion" filled the meeting room to capacity.

The speaker was thrilled with the turnout. "I wish I could think of a word to describe it," he said.

From the back of the room an agent boomed, "Mandatory."

While we might chuckle at that speaker's misunderstanding of his popularity, unhappy consequences can result when we presume we know all the facts about situations that affect us negatively. I have to ask myself, how many times have I made assumptions without first getting to know a person's unique set of circumstances? I confess I've done it often. If people don't treat me right, I've been known to jump to conclusions about their motives instead of praying for them and giving them the benefit of the doubt. But as the Gospel of Luke reminds me, only Jesus knows what people are thinking. I'm a lot better off when I don't assume too much.

Remembering that important truth will probably increase my chances of contentment by at least 56 percent.

Lord, forgive me for lumping everyone together
and assuming I know why they act as they
do. May your marvelous grace and mercy flow
through me to help them heal, even as you are
healing me from my own wounds. Amen.

32

The Divine Supervac

Listen to my prayer, O God...
My thoughts trouble me and I am distraught.

PSALM 55:1-2

Ewww!" My daughter backed away from the corner of the storage room where she'd just picked up a box. Under the carton was undeniable evidence of a rodent invasion. She had reason to recoil. Mice can carry hantavirus—and she was pregnant.

I ran for the Shop-Vac. While the machine did the dirty work, I carefully guided the hose so unintended items weren't also inhaled along with mouse droppings.

Vacuum cleaners don't differentiate. They'll suck up anything they get close to, whether it's doo-doo, dirt, or diamonds. If not emptied soon, the contents hibernate together inside the bag or canister, a perfect environment for bacteria, mold, and other nasty organisms to proliferate.

People can be like vacuum cleaners. Whatever we absorb takes up residence inside us. Our minds can fill with goopy resentment and shards of broken intentions. But the good news is, we can ask God to dump it all out and make us clean again.

Centuries before vacuum cleaners, King David offered this prayer:

> Search me, God, and know my heart;
>   test me and know my anxious thoughts.
> See if there is any offensive way in me,

and lead me in the way everlasting
(Psalm 139:23-24).

David didn't want to fill up with anxious worries or offensive ways. He also knew it was futile to try to hide secret thoughts from the Omniscient One. Amazingly, knowing everything about us doesn't prevent God from loving us anyway.

O Lord, you have examined my heart
and know everything about me.
You know when I sit down or stand up.
You know my thoughts even when I'm far away.
You see me when I travel
and when I rest at home.
You know everything I do.
You know what I am going to say
even before I say it, Lord...
Such knowledge is too wonderful for me,
too great for me to understand!...
How precious are your thoughts about me, O God.
They cannot be numbered!
I can't even count them;
they outnumber the grains of sand!
(Psalm 139:1-4,6,17-18 NLT).

If you grew up believing that God watches for every infraction so he can slap you down, David's statements may seem too good to be true. As I've emerged from that former mindset, I've discovered the joy of serving a God who knows all about me yet loves me anyway—and even more important, *likes* me anyway.

The enemy of our souls would like us to think that contamination by the doo-doo of this world automatically disqualifies us from being worthy of our heavenly Father's loving attention. That belief not only keeps us from fulfilling our God-given potential but also devalues the cleansing power of Christ.

Remember, we can safely trust God's probing and cleansing in our lives. When we confess our trespasses, we guide the vacuum hose to where it should go. I can think of no greater blessing than having my sins removed while God assures me my worth is far greater than diamonds—no matter where they're scattered.

Lord Jesus, owner and operator of the Divine
Supervac, thank you for being willing and able
to cleanse me from all my sins. Amen.

33

Taking a Bite out of Worry

So do not worry, saying, "What shall we eat?" or
"What shall we drink?" or "What shall we wear?" For...
your heavenly Father knows that you need them.

MATTHEW 6:31-32

A couple of my dental fillings need to be replaced. You wouldn't think that fact alone would plunge me into a funk, even though keeping my mouth wide open for an hour isn't my idea of a merry time. But it's not just the dental visit itself. It's also the cost. Fillings and porcelain crowns aren't cheap.

That worry ushers in other financial concerns and reminds me of my shrinking emergency fund. Before I know it, I'm imagining all sorts of dire crises that will mire me in debt.

I've been down this road before, so I know I need to…

- …take myself by the scruff of the neck and quote applicable Scripture verses—out loud so my ears can hear them. (Living alone has its advantages.) Each time I say, "My God will meet all your needs according to the riches of his glory in Christ Jesus" (Philippians 4:19), the truth sinks deeper into my spirit.

- …remind myself that even though my emotions haven't caught up with the truth yet, reality hasn't changed. Of course, I shouldn't stuff my emotions. But they do form powerful filters through which I experience reality. I can't rely on emotions to give me the unvarnished truth.

- …count my blessings. When depression threatens to descend, nothing lifts me like being consciously grateful. I may have experienced significant losses in life, but I'm also a very blessed woman. Just having a roof over my head, clothes to wear, food to eat, and safe drinking water means I'm richer than a large percentage of the world's population.

Having teeth that need attention puts me in a privileged class. Some people's only dental option is to have bad teeth pulled. That toothless image reminds me how much I have to be thankful for.

Dear God, thanks for teeth, dentists, fillings, and the power of gratitude to straighten out my emotions. And when it comes to getting truth down into my spirit, I'm glad your Word has...teeth to it. Amen.

34

Electrifying Storms

You have been a refuge for the poor,
a refuge for the needy in their distress,
a shelter from the storm
and a shade from the heat.

ISAIAH 25:4

Scientists warn people not to use their cell phones outdoors during thunderstorms because of the risk of being struck by lightning. A comedian has added that you should also avoid using them in movie theaters because of the risk of being strangled.

In a manner of speaking, Benjamin Franklin shares some of the blame for those particular cell-phone dangers. In 1752, when he flew a kite during a thunderstorm and proved that lightning and electricity were the same thing, he moved us a step closer to being able to harness electricity's power and invent every electronic gadget that now clutters the planet.

Centuries before Benjamin Franklin's storm-time activities, the disciples were electrified in a different sense in the middle of the Sea of Galilee. While they were disturbed by the wind-whipped waves slapping their boat, what really stood their hair on end was seeing Jesus walk on the choppy water. They were sure he was a ghost.

Bold-spirited Peter knew how to determine what they were dealing with. "Lord, if it's you," he called out, "tell me to come to you on the water" (Matthew 14:28). Jesus gave the invitation, and Peter actually climbed out of the boat and took a few steps on the lake's surface. But when he focused more on the storm's power than on

God's power, he began to sink. Peter survived because the Lord reached out his hand and caught him.

"A Shelter in the Time of Storm," a venerable gospel song from a previous century, reminds us God is our refuge in every situation:

> The raging storms may round us beat,
> A Shelter in the time of storm;
> We'll never leave our safe retreat,
> A Shelter in the time of storm.
>
> Oh, Jesus is a Rock in a weary land,
> A weary land, a weary land;
> Oh, Jesus is a Rock in a weary land,
> A Shelter in the time of storm. [1]

Are you being battered by storms? Are you in danger of sinking under waves of tragedy or being struck by lightning-hot calamities? Whatever impending disaster threatens to overwhelm you, remember, when you call on God, he will be your secure refuge.

Unless, of course, you try calling him on your cell phone in a movie theater.

> *Lord, thank you for bringing me safely through*
> *every storm in life and for giving me courage*
> *in the face of danger. You are my secure refuge.*
> *Help me trust in you completely. Amen.*

35

Dremeling Out New Spaces

He brought me out into a spacious place.

PSALM 18:19

When I inherited a 23-year-old 1983 Dodge Colt, its odometer had only 48,000 original miles on it. The car hadn't been out of my grandmother's yard in years. I had to invest in several hundred dollars' worth of new rubber, filters, spark plugs, radiator flushing, brakes, and more before I could drive it on the freeway.

Grandpa had ordered a stripped-down version when he bought it new from the factory. He dubbed the vehicle "PJ," for Plain Jane. I tried to be grateful for basic transportation that got me from point A to point B. It came with no monthly loan payments. The subcompact could squeeze into tight parking spaces, and it was so old it no longer needed biannual emissions testing in our county. But I also reminded the Lord that in my next automobile, I'd appreciate intermittent wipers, a right-side rearview mirror, and something fancier than the original AM radio.

Five years after I received the car, God answered my stereo request. The adventure began when the radio stopped working every minute or two. My handywoman sister volunteered to take a look. "It's toast," she declared. "You need a new one."

At the big-box store, choices overwhelmed me. It seems no one sells plain AM radios anymore. We ended up with a combination AM/FM radio, CD player, and MP3/WMA player featuring Bluetooth capability and a USB port.

The new unit was bigger than the old one, so we attacked the faceplate that had been part of the original molded dash. Once my sister made the final cut with a Dremel handheld rotary tool, she said, "We're committed now!"

Hoping she was referring to the need to complete the task and not that we were about to be carted off to a home for the bewildered, I thought about the courage it takes to acknowledge that old ways have ceased to be viable. And how important it is to move forward, even when we're afraid.

I could have left the old radio in and simply never used it. But taking a risk resulted in a functional stereo system that assured me of traffic and weather reports, music to keep me alert, and hands-free cell-phone use in emergencies.

Risks never come with guarantees, even when we seek God's direction. Each new venture requires courage. Perhaps that's what gives me empathy for emotionally wounded people. I understand how frightening it can be to leave one's comfort zone. I know change can seem even scarier than remaining in one's current painful situation.

When Jesus warned his disciples not to put new wine into old wineskins because fermentation would burst the stretched-out leather, he wasn't giving a tutorial on winemaking. He was talking about spiritual matters (see Matthew 9, Mark 2, and Luke 5). If he had preached to today's crowds, perhaps his admonition would be to refrain from shoving high-tech audio systems into spaces intended for 28-year-old AM radios—at least until we make enlargements.

As we advance in the healing process, we need enlarged spaces for the increased power and bevy of options God is equipping us with. Now…let's rock our world.

Lord Jesus, thank you for expanded room to grow
so I can experience life to the full. Help me never
to settle for cramped spaces again. Amen.

36

Having Our Cake

*Blessed are those who hunger and thirst for
righteousness, for they will be filled.*

MATTHEW 5:6

A newspaper publisher provided snacks for staff members who worked through the night to produce the paper's morning edition. At about 6:30 a.m. one day, a hungry employee turned to the city editor and asked, "Is there any more food?"

"Yeah, I think there's some cake left," was the reply. "But you can't have your cake and edit too."

When I need to eat, my family notices it right away because I get grumpy. It's not due to any specific medical condition. My body simply needs healthy nourishment every four hours or so. If I don't get it, the world changes before my eyes. People annoy me. I can't think how to answer their silly questions. I want everyone just to go away and leave me alone. At those times, it's amazing what a dab of peanut butter on whole-grain toast or some nonfat yogurt with fresh fruit and nuts can do for my outlook.

Our souls need healthy nutrition too. Otherwise, our spiritual edge deteriorates; we can't hear God's voice as clearly, and we're not as well equipped to minister to others around us. But many people hold back from indulging in God's spiritual feast. Some have been poisoned by false teaching. Others were burned by manipulation or deceit. It's difficult for them to trust again.

My friend Agnes Lawless Elkins and her late husband, John Lawless, thought they never could become deceived. They had been

Christians all their lives. They had studied at well-known Bible colleges and universities and even spent seven years overseas with a respected mission organization. But that was no guarantee of safety.

"In all good faith," Agnes says, "we got caught in an aberrant church and drifted with the rest of its members towards the shoals of deception. We learned that such groups are a growing menace and use cultlike methods to draw and control adherents." In her book *The Drift into Deception: The Eight Characteristics of Abusive Christianity*, Agnes likens their experience to being on Lake Erie when an excursion boat loses its rudder control and drifts toward Niagara Falls. Instead of calling for help, the captain hides the seriousness of the situation from the passengers. When a man on a nearby boat shouts a warning, the captain assures passengers nothing is wrong. Eventually the boat plunges over the falls and breaks to pieces on rocks below. [1]

Agnes and John learned that even devout Christians can drift into deception if they ignore the winds of false doctrine and tolerate controlling behaviors by spiritual leaders. Each of us is vulnerable.

The prophet Jeremiah gives voice to wounded believers:

> We hoped for peace—
>   nothing good came from it;
> we looked for healing—
>   and got kicked in the stomach (Jeremiah 14:19 MSG).

Who feels like coming to the table after that kind of treatment?

Fortunately, God understands traumatized souls. He also understands that hunger pangs don't go away just because we've been injured. Jesus promises that if we hunger and thirst for righteousness, he will completely fill us. But we must risk trusting him again, even when our injuries came from people claiming to speak and act on his behalf.

God does not authorize spiritual abuse. He is never happy when anyone is wounded in faith communities. When we've suffered that kind of treatment, we must not allow ourselves to be separated from the compassionate God of hope, who fills us with all joy and peace as we trust in him (Romans 15:13). It is because of God's tender mercies that we can be confident he will satisfy us with good things (Psalm 103:5).

The good news is, we can have our cake—and healing too.

Lord Jesus, thank you for safely satisfying my spiritual
appetite when I hunger and thirst for you. Amen.

37

Hope for Nobodies

I hope you will put up with me in a little foolishness.

2 CORINTHIANS 11:1

While browsing in a crafts store, a couple noticed a number of country-style musical instruments, including flutes, dulcimers, and recorders. The husband picked up a one-stringed instrument he assumed to be a mouth harp, put it to his lips, and twanged a few notes.

His wife, who had wandered to another aisle, hurried past several amused shoppers to reach her husband. "I'm sorry to tell you this, honey," she whispered, "but you're trying to play a cheese slicer."

Since this man shared his embarrassing moment in a national magazine, it's clear he could laugh at himself. I, on the other hand, grew up believing that admitting mistakes was never a good idea.

Many of my spiritual mentors must have been baptized in pickle juice. They'd memorized every Bible verse that mentions foolishness, and if anyone doubted the importance of a serious outlook on life, those mentors referred to 1 Peter 5:8, which stresses being alert and of sober mind. They also quoted Isaiah 53:3 (KJV), which says that Jesus was "despised and rejected of men; a man of sorrows, and acquainted with grief." Of course, everyone knew we were supposed to be like Jesus (see Romans 8:29, 2 Corinthians 3:18, and Galatians 4:19). So obviously, we should focus on sorrow and ignore all the Bible verses that speak of rejoicing. (In my circles, the term *Christian comedian* was an oxymoron.)

My views have improved a lot since childhood, but every so

often, another opportunity comes along to work on my ability to laugh at myself. One example is when I traded in my 1983 Dodge Colt for a 1992 Toyota Corolla (which was 19 years old at the time). The night was clear when I climbed into my "new" car to drive it home. I turned the key in the ignition, and as soon as the engine started, the rear-window wiper came on.

I made a quick cell-phone call to the previous owners. I was told, "Just twist the end of the wiper wand." For the next ten miles, I twisted, pulled, and jiggled the wiper wand until my wrist was sore, but the mechanism continued to swipe away, flagging every vehicle behind me: "Yoo hoo! Watch out for the clueless driver."

I remained calm by focusing on how soon I could duck into my garage and turn off the vehicle's power. Then, two miles from my house, an accident up ahead forced me to take a long detour through the south part of town. The wiper blade scraped dry glass the entire way. Only later did I learn that the rear wiper's switch was on the opposite side of the dash from the wiper wand.

Throughout my childhood, I rarely saw people close to me laugh at personal mistakes, but I heard plenty of criticism when others faltered. That set me up to believe I needed to get an A-plus on every commandment and rule.

Fortunately, as a recovering perfectionist, I am able now to laugh at myself a whole lot more than I used to. So by the time I got the Corolla home, I'd almost convinced myself it didn't really matter what other drivers thought. *Maybe I've even provided some amusement at dinner tables around town*, I thought. Moms and dads, home from a grueling workday, could entertain their children: "You wouldn't believe the dumb blonde I was following tonight."

While I have no desire to supply that kind of entertainment on a regular basis, I do love how God brings glory to himself as the result of our failures. Paul explained:

> The Message that points to Christ on the Cross seems
> like sheer silliness to those hellbent on destruction, but

for those on the way of salvation it makes perfect sense. This is the way God works, and most powerfully as it turns out (1 Corinthians 1:18 MSG).

Yes, sometimes I struggle to believe that God could use my quirks and frailties in any positive way. But God's Word trumps early training. As my thoughts line up with the truth, I focus on my new freedom instead of dwelling on years lost to emotional bondage.

Paul continued:

> Take a good look, friends, at who you were when you got called into this life. I don't see many of "the brightest and the best" among you, not many influential, not many from high-society families. Isn't it obvious that God deliberately chose men and women that the culture overlooks and exploits and abuses, chose these "nobodies" to expose the hollow pretensions of the "somebodies"? (1 Corinthians 1:26-28 MSG).

Although an older relative of mine was a vibrant, churchgoing believer, he never became an official church member. After his death, I learned he'd been divorced twice before coming to Christ. Divorced people were marginalized in his denomination, so he kept his background a Deep Dark Secret. Even though his third marriage lasted more than 50 years, he couldn't bring himself to fill out the membership application that inquired about former spouses. Most likely the church would have accepted him into membership, but his opportunities for ministry would have been severely restricted. So, he found an outlet for service through a parachurch ministry that didn't pry into his past.

Regardless of that loved one's previous mistakes, he touched many lives through his love and faithfulness. Our family "nobody" did indeed put to shame the hollow pretensions of the "somebodies" who would have judged him.

I'm grateful God has the power to change the pretensions I

was taught in my formative years. I'm even getting a little better at admitting my own imperfections. The fact that I'm going public with the wiper-blade story reveals how far I've come.

Keep that in mind if you ever see me trying to coax a tune out of a cheese slicer.

Gracious God, thank you for setting me and all of your
children free from unbiblical mindsets about humor,
our frailties, and your forgiving nature. Amen.

38

Catch-22 Expeditions

To search out a matter is the glory of kings.

PROVERBS 25:2

The garage smelled terrible, so my sister went on a hunt for the cause. Not only was she familiar with that particular odor, but gnaw-marks on items in storage also gave her a clue. She told me a few days later, "I found the dead rat. I'm both happy and disgusted."

She'd been on a catch-22 expedition. Failure meant a persistent stench, and success meant dealing with a decaying carcass.

Decaying faith can also be stinky. One by-product of life's wounding experiences is what I call *spiritual necrosis*. When emotional scars restrict the flow of God's life-giving power long enough, we experience the death of spiritual tissue. Eventually, gangrene of the soul can set in.

We're usually more alert to the odor of decay in others than we are to our own rottenness. It's like the man who discovered a pair of his son's smelly sneakers on the kitchen table. "Doesn't he know how disgusting that is?" he complained to his wife. The man dropped the shoes by the back door and went outside to work on a car while his wife left in their other vehicle to get groceries.

When she returned later, she couldn't find a place to put the grocery bags because a carburetor was sitting in the middle of the kitchen table.

Instead of being concerned only about the status of others, it's important to keep tabs on the state of our own spiritual health, as the apostle Paul urges:

Test yourselves to make sure you are solid in the faith. Don't drift along taking everything for granted. Give yourselves regular checkups. You need firsthand evidence, not mere hearsay, that Jesus Christ is in you. Test it out. If you fail the test, do something about it (2 Corinthians 13:5 MSG).

Expeditions of this sort can be unpleasant, but the rewards are certainly gratifying. After all, the writer of Proverbs 25 declares it is the glory of kings to search things out. Wouldn't you like to be a member of that royalty and expose any rats of abuse, doubt, or sin that have gnawed holes in your faith? What you find and remove may be disgusting, but the vibrancy that returns to your spiritual life will make the effort more than worthwhile.

And you'll come out smelling like a rose.

Lord, search my heart for any resident rats I need to get rid of or chewed areas that need restoration. I want to experience the full flow of your life-giving power. Amen.

39

Paying Attention to Names

The nations will see your vindication,
and all kings your glory;
you will be called by a new name
that the mouth of the LORD will bestow.

ISAIAH 62:2

I recently re-watched the 1940 movie *His Girl Friday*. Known for its rapid-fire dialogue, it takes several viewings to catch all the funny lines and in-jokes.

Archibald Leach, known to moviegoers as Cary Grant, plays the role of newspaper editor Walter Burns. His star reporter, Hildy Johnson (Rosalind Russell) is engaged to Bruce Baldwin, played by well-known actor Ralph Bellamy.

Conniving to get Hildy back to the newspaper, Walter cooks up a scheme that involves unsuspecting Bruce and a blonde vamp. As he tells the blonde what to do, she asks what Bruce looks like. Walter responds, "That guy in the movies, Ralph Bellamy."

Later, a crooked politician threatens Walter. "Whistling in the dark won't help," sneers the bad guy. "You're through."

Unfazed, Cary Grant's character utters another of the movie's in-jokes: "Archie Leach said that to me a week before he cut his throat."

We writers pay attention to names. We carefully christen our fiction characters and give pseudonyms to nonfiction characters whose identities we want to protect. What we call someone usually conveys gender and often implies age, nationality, and even meaning.

Names also go in and out of fashion. After reading the list of

121

all 264 graduates in my niece Ariel's high-school commencement program a couple of years ago, I recognized only Ariel and her best friend. I also noticed that the name Mackenzie must have been popular for girls born 18 years previously. I spotted three of them with various spellings—four, if you count middle names—along with one Kenzie.

In Bible times, names carried significant meanings. Isaac means "laughter" in Hebrew (Genesis 21:5-7). Melchizedek means "king of righteousness" (Hebrews 7:2). When Abigail made her case to King David, she said, "Please pay no attention, my lord, to that wicked man Nabal. He is just like his name—his name means Fool" (1 Samuel 25:25).

Scripture also mentions numerous people who were renamed. An Egyptian pharaoh changed Joseph's name to Zaphenath-Paneah. King Nebuchadnezzar changed Daniel's name to Belteshazzar. God changed names to reflect a new significance in people's lives: Abram to Abraham, Sarai to Sarah, Jacob to Israel, Simon to Peter...

My sister chose the name Ariel for her daughter because it means "lioness of God," not because of Disney's key character in *The Little Mermaid,* as most people assume.

Do you know what your name means? You don't have to be pigeonholed by traditional meanings listed on name-the-baby websites. The meaning of my name, Diana—"goddess of hunting" and "goddess of the moon"—does not thrill me. However, I decided that just as the moon reflects the light of the sun, so also I can choose to reflect the light of God's Son. Now, although my name hasn't actually changed, it does have a new, purposeful meaning for me.

Using the same principle, we can recast ourselves from victim to overcomer. The change doesn't happen overnight. But it *will* take place through God's unconditional love and abundant grace if we are willing to trust him enough to allow him to do the work. God not only changes us into new creations when we become believers

(2 Corinthians 5:17) but also gives each of us a new name (Revelation 2:17).

And you don't have to look like anyone in the movies to experience that transformation.

> *Loving God, thank you for what's new in my life—*
> *my name, my spiritual destination, and my state of*
> *healing. Help me to recognize the same new beginning*
> *you give to others, even when it's hard to let go of*
> *past hurts and disappointments. With your help, I*
> *will fulfill the meaning of my new name. Amen.*

PART FOUR

Pursuing Possibilities

We have come to one of the most important heart lifters—learning to pursue new possibilities in life regardless of what we've been through. That includes letting go of misconceptions, such as was illustrated at a restaurant when a woman and her husband were toasting their fourteenth wedding anniversary. They noticed a similar scene taking place at the next table between a man and woman who looked to be in their seventies.

The younger woman smiled at the older couple, whom she was sure had enjoyed a long, happy union. "We've been married for fourteen years," she confided to them. "How long have you been together?"

The older man hesitated for a second and then replied, "Actually, we're celebrating having met one week ago today."

Having our expectations overturned can be delightful, but all too often our preconceived ideas can shackle us to incorrect assumptions and attitudes that veer us off course. When we allow God to reveal to us life's possibilities, we can shed victim mentalities, forgive those who hurt us, develop attitudes of gratitude, show compassion to ourselves and others, roll our burdens onto the Lord, and adopt the goal of living up to a new purpose.

So lift your glass with me in a toast to the pursuit of possibilities whether you've recently discovered new vistas or are still developing a worldview you've been enjoying for decades. Searching out potentialities is part of the abundant life God had in mind for us from the beginning.

40

God's Special Effects

You were taught...to be made new in
the attitude of your minds.

Ephesians 4:22-23

As a mother and her young daughter sat buckled in their seats near the airplane's wing, the mom explained that they were flying over the ocean. "Can you see the water?" she asked.

"No," said the girl, peering out the window at the wing. "But I can see the diving board."

When the people of Israel escaped Egypt after 430 years of slavery only to be caught between the Red Sea and Egypt's army, I wonder if some of them felt like looking for a diving board.

Our pastor once referred in his sermon to that historical time as he got ready to show a video clip from the classic *The Ten Commandments*. "Don't laugh," he said. "Although the scene is a serious one, I had to hold back a chuckle when I previewed it."

We gazed expectantly at a screen above the platform. Charlton Heston appeared in his famous role of Moses, having just led the descendants of the patriarch Jacob (Israel) out of Egypt. But now the people were trapped "between the devil and the deep blue sea."

I've always loved director Cecil B. DeMille's interpretation of immense saltwater walls on either side of an ocean-floor path. However, viewing the movie clip nearly six decades after its release, I could see why the pastor was amused. Computer-generated imagery (CGI) is vastly superior to the special effects available back in 1956.

I'm glad the message of hope hasn't changed, however. God still delivers his people when we call upon him. The Israelites had already seen their divine deliverer use plagues to convince the Egyptians to let them go. But the Israelites' first bump on freedom's road revealed how deeply mired they were in a victim mentality. Instead of believing that God would rescue them again, they were ready to hightail it right back into bondage. They whined to Moses:

> Was it because there were no graves in Egypt that you brought us to the desert to die? What have you done to us by bringing us out of Egypt? Didn't we say to you in Egypt, "Leave us alone; let us serve the Egyptians"? It would have been better for us to serve the Egyptians than to die in the desert! (Exodus 14:11-12).

God created an escape route in spite of their bad attitudes, and from the safety of the opposite shore, the former slaves watched the mysteriously piled-up water collapse on top of Pharaoh's army. In response, God's people danced and sang songs of praise.

Three days later, the two million or so adults and children, along with their livestock, faced a second dilemma involving water. This time, instead of having too much, they had too little. But rather than appeal to Almighty God, the people ramped up their complaints. Still, the Lord provided drinkable water. Their faith failed again a short time later when they ran out of food. And so it went. Throughout their trek, they always found something to grumble about. Their fears and their failure to trust God's provision kept them out of the Promised Land for 40 years.

Today, our spiritual journey can be just as difficult. Each of us encounters darkness, storms, washouts, steep inclines, temperature extremes, and even predators. We can do little about external elements, but we *can* remain in control of our attitudes. It boils down to this: Will we choose to trust God, or will we complain? The wise choice, of course, is to trust in the Lord, even when enemies advance.

God responds to our faith, often with such spectacular miracles of provision that CGI pales by comparison.

And that's even more exciting than diving boards on airplanes.

> *Almighty God, thank you for freeing me from spiritual slavery, for guiding me on my wilderness trek, and for supernaturally meeting my needs, time and again. Help me to maintain right attitudes so I won't miss out on the land of delights that you've promised. Amen.*

41

Don't Want No Crabby People

In the morning, LORD, you hear my voice.

PSALM 5:3

Leaving my cousin's house while the desert sun still slept, we drove for 40 minutes to a dark park-and-ride lot. We stood in line with hundreds of other people waiting for a shuttle to take us to Albuquerque's International Balloon Fiesta.

As minutes passed, the long lines hardly moved. Then just before seven a.m., someone investigated the delay and reported that according to a sign, shuttle service would cease in five minutes.

General grumbling ensued. One person, noting campaign posters for a mayoral election the following week, said, "If the incumbent really wants to get reelected, he should hand out free coffee and apologies."

"Yeah," another chimed in. "And if his opponent promised that this would never happen on his watch, he'd be a shoo-in."

I'd been trying to look on the bright side—or at least find something to alleviate our boredom. Then I spotted out-of-state license plates on many parked cars. Tourists had come from Arizona, Colorado, Illinois, Washington State, Texas—even other countries—for the balloon festival. They had gathered from great distances because of similar interests. "That'll be just like heaven," I chirped to my sister, my cousin, and his fiancée.

Then I thought of the poor hobbit, Bilbo Baggins, rushing off on an adventure without his hat, walking stick, or even a pocket handkerchief. "We, on the other hand, have tissues, beautiful weather, and porta-potties nearby," I said, fishing out some Chapstick to replenish my dry lips and offering hand lotion to my sister. Neither she nor I were used to such low humidity. She shook her head and took a long sip of coffee from her insulated mug.

Instead of closing down shuttle service at seven, authorities commandeered school buses to help with transportation. I lost no time in pointing out that although we'd miss the initial launch, we could look forward to seeing hot-air balloons after all.

My night-owl sister, up since four a.m., had listened to me blather on like Pollyanna long enough. She took one last sip of coffee and peered at me through bloodshot eyes. "Do you have to talk so much this early in the morning?"

At first I was stunned. I'd intended to help the situation, not make it worse. But then I remembered Proverbs 27:14 (NLT): "A loud and cheerful greeting early in the morning will be taken as a curse!" My poor sister!

So, I zipped my lip.

When we finally climbed aboard a shuttle, the driver greeted us with enthusiasm. She wore outlandish makeup, enormous hoop earrings, and a Julia Roberts smile. "I don't want no crabby people on my bus!" she announced, vigorously shifting into gear.

Another morning person! I felt vindicated. If anyone could redeem the day, it would be our driver. She was better than a triple grande mocha for those whose spirits needed perking up. When we filed off the bus 30 minutes later, everyone gave her a rousing *hip hip hooray*. Evidently it was no longer too early in the morning for such cheerfulness.

We immersed ourselves at the fiesta. Actually, we had little choice because the packed crowd moved us down the field like so many busy corpuscles in one giant artery. We visited vendors' booths. We watched striped and checkerboard balloons sail in the frigid sunshine, jockeying for space with airborne clowns, frogs, cows, witches, devils, daisies, houses, pigs, ladybugs, cacti, chipmunks, and bumblebees holding hands—not to mention the occasional soccer ball and football balloon. It was exhausting. We reinforced ourselves with more coffee and New Mexican-style breakfast burritos. After two hours of frivolity, we were ready to go home.

This time we remained in the shuttle line for 90 minutes. Several hundred yards away, a police helicopter landed. My cousin's fiancée suggested that someone behind us in line was "going postal" due to the delay. Festival officials sent a juggler to entertain us as we shuffled along.

In exchange for two hours of balloon watching, we spent nearly six hours waiting in line and commuting.

Doesn't that sound like life in general? For many people, daily living is nothing more than long stretches of boredom punctuated by periods of overload. No matter where you are in that cycle, I'm still convinced that one of the best coping mechanisms available is choosing to adopt a good attitude.

Just don't verbalize it too early in the morning.

> *Lord, I'm so grateful that your children can count on your help whether we're morning people, night owls, or somewhere in the middle. I'm glad you hear my prayers no matter what time of day or night I call on you. Amen.*

42

Showing Ourselves Compassion

*But you are a forgiving God, gracious and
compassionate, slow to anger and abounding in love.*

NEHEMIAH 9:17

Teena took numerous snapshots at her friend's ninety-ninth birthday party and then showed them to the guest of honor. "Good grief," the older woman said as she reviewed the photos. "I look like I'm a hundred."

That woman needed self-compassion. Just like a lot of the rest of us. Too often our spirits have been beaten down by emphasis on our sinful natures and unworthiness. Hymnals have us sing about being wretches and worms. Scriptures seem to support those images:

- "For all have sinned, and come short of the glory of God" (Romans 3:23 KJV).

- "There is no one righteous, not even one" (Romans 3:10).

- "The heart is deceitful above all things, and desperately wicked: who can know it?" (Jeremiah 17:9 KJV).

These verses do explain why each of us needs a Redeemer, but if we don't also consider other verses in the Bible, we end up with an unbalanced view.

Compassion for ourselves means we're as kind and understanding about our own shortcomings as we are about a friend's. It's important to let go of debilitating self-criticism so we can offset its negative effects and learn to be kind to ourselves. When we are able to put an end to destructive emotional patterns, we'll end up healthier, happier, and more effective in everything we do.

Some Christians have been taught to be suspicious of secular psychologists and self-help gurus. I've heard more than one preacher use handpicked Bible verses about humanity's depravity to counter such psychological concepts as self-esteem. However, while God's Word is always true, our understanding will be out of balance if we focus only on our sinful natures. Here are examples of what else Scripture says about how God sees and interacts with us:

- God is gracious, compassionate, and abounding in love and faithfulness; he forgives our transgressions, wickedness, and rebellion; he freely pardons sin and delights to show mercy; his love endures forever (see Exodus 34:6-7; Nehemiah 9:17; Psalm 103:8; 106:1; Isaiah 55:7; Joel 2:13; Micah 7:18). The Lord rejoices over us with singing (see Zephaniah 3:17).

- If we confess our sins, God will forgive us our sins and purify us from all unrighteousness (see 1 John 1:9).

- Each of us is far more valuable than sheep, birds, and many sparrows (see Matthew 12:11-12; Luke 12:6-7,24).

- Because of his great love for us, God, who is rich in mercy, made us alive, raised us up, and seated us in the heavenly realms in Christ Jesus in order that he might show the incomparable riches of his grace expressed in his kindness to us in Christ Jesus. We're God's handiwork, created in Christ Jesus, and prepared in advance to do good works (see Ephesians 2:4-10).

- God's nature is love. He calls us his children, and we can rely on the great love he lavishes on us (see 1 John 3:1; 4:9-10,16).

Considering the tremendous mercy God shows us, what right

do we have to deny ourselves compassion? Agreeing with God doesn't mean we think we're better than anyone else or that we've done anything to earn God's favor. It simply means we're not going to let Satan keep us bound in condemnation any longer. God created us so we could have a relationship with him. Acknowledging his gift of compassion honors that relationship.

Let's just not wait until our ninety-ninth birthday party to accept it.

> *Loving heavenly Father, thank you for revealing in*
> *Scripture why I should show myself compassion. I*
> *can't boast that I've earned the right to view myself*
> *that way; I simply agree with how you've chosen to*
> *look at every person. I'm deeply grateful. Amen.*

43

Allergic to Grasshoppers

He gave their crops to the grasshopper.

PSALM 78:46

Recently I decided to cook up some wheat kernels that I'd acquired directly from a farm in Eastern Washington. That meant I had to pick out dried grasshopper parts before measuring the grain into a cooking pot.

Calling them "natural contaminants," the US Food and Drug Administration (FDA) allows certain levels of insects, rodent hairs, and other disgusting matter in our food supply. I was distressed to learn that even *chocolate* is contaminated! Evidently putting up with contaminants is our only alternative to being poisoned by excessive amounts of pesticide, since cleaning by hand would be prohibitively expensive. One university study estimates that the average American eats from one to two pounds of insects each year without knowing it.

If the thought nauseates you, maybe it's because of your nationality. Boiled and salted grasshoppers are routinely sun dried for snacks in the Middle East. In certain African countries, they're added to soup. Some Chinese food markets serve the insects on skewers. Mexicans spice up grasshoppers with garlic, onions, and chilies and then drench the entire dish in lime juice.

In the United States, boxes of chocolate-covered insects are sold as novelties only—thus lending a whole new meaning to the term *gag gift*.

Most consumers prefer not to think about food contaminants,

but some individuals can't simply ignore them. Judy Tidwell, a specialist at a state social-services office in the southeastern United States, knows firsthand that people with allergies and asthma can experience stomach disorders and other maladies when they ingest such material. In other words, bugs in their dinner literally make them sick. What is acceptable for the majority of the population brings harm to a minority.

For too long we've overlooked a similar issue in faith communities. Guidelines based on religious traditions and various interpretations of Scripture fit most situations quite well. But when unique factors exist, not everyone is willing to consider making exceptions.

I know individuals who tried to reach out for help when parents, spouses, or religious leaders abused them in some way. Unfortunately, those to whom they appealed were squeamish or perhaps felt unequipped to deal with messy situations. So, without giving equal importance to what the Bible says about God's hatred of violence and ill-treatment, they instructed victims to heed the general mandates of turning the other cheek, honoring parents, obeying one's husband, and submitting to church leaders. The victims, like the minority susceptible to insect parts, suffered toxic reactions.

I'm not trying to be critical of leaders. In my previous leadership roles, I didn't always know whom to believe when people told me their situations. Every story has at least two sides. Sometimes innocent people are falsely accused.

But we must acknowledge that in the melee, people have been wounded. Instead of receiving spiritual first aid, many of them have been ignored or given the wrong prescriptions. So, although victims still may worship God, they often stop going to church, where they fear further wounding. In their pain, they might self-medicate with food, alcohol, drugs, or questionable behaviors. They know we suspect their motives. They hear us call them backsliders. They are aware that sometimes we disguise gossip as public prayer requests when we say they "aren't walking with the Lord" or refer to them as having "left the ministry."

These issues are complicated. However, it's vital to give struggling Christians a voice. We must consider serving as Good Samaritans to those who've been spiritually assaulted and left to die along the way.

To differentiate legitimate needs from fabricated ones, we must rely on the Holy Spirit's guidance in each situation. If we're not sure we hear God's clear direction, we can choose in the meantime to show mercy while maintaining personal boundaries so we don't fall victim to "allergic reactions" ourselves.

This is how the apostle Paul explained it to the first-century church in Galatia:

> Live creatively, friends. If someone falls into sin, forgivingly restore him, saving your critical comments for yourself. You might be needing forgiveness before the day's out. Stoop down and reach out to those who are oppressed. Share their burdens, and so complete Christ's law. If you think you are too good for that, you are badly deceived (Galatians 6:1-3 MSG).

Instead of scolding wounded Christians for "forsaking the assembling" of themselves together with other believers (Hebrews 10:25 KJV), we can remind them that God understands their pain and desires to maintain a loving relationship with them. He alone sees all the hurts in a person's life and perfectly understands allergic reactions to the contaminants he or she has been forced to ingest. Wounded people need time to heal and trust again.

You never know when your compassion may be the very antidote that helps people return to spiritual wholeness.

Just don't include a box of chocolates.

*Compassionate heavenly Father, grant me divine
wisdom in reaching out to the "allergic minority." Only
you can see clearly into each complicated situation.
Help me know the right way to respond. Amen.*

44

The Allure of Disability

"Lord," they answered, "we want our sight."
Jesus had compassion on them and touched their eyes.

MATTHEW 20:33-34

As the story goes, three guys are on a lake fishing when Jesus appears in their boat. The first man recovers from shock and says, "I've suffered from back pain for years. Would you please heal me?" Jesus touches the man's back, and instantly the pain is gone.

The second man removes his Coke-bottle glasses and asks Jesus to cure his poor eyesight. Jesus flings the eyeglasses overboard. Immediately, the man's vision clears, and he sees everything perfectly.

Jesus now turns to the third man, who throws up his hands in alarm. "Don't touch me!" he cries. "I'm on disability!"

While it's normal to want to be well, perhaps you know those who choose to remain in a victim mode. Instead of using difficult life experiences as stepping-stones to greater maturity and wisdom, they prefer to wallow in their losses. The crutch of impairment allows them to avoid taking responsibility for their own lives while they drain sympathy and energy from those around them.

The Gospel of Matthew tells us about two men who eagerly sought deliverance. On the side of a road leaving Jericho, they cried out, asking Jesus to have mercy on them. Jesus responded by asking specifically what they wanted him to do. "We want our sight," they said. He touched their eyes, and they were healed immediately.

I love the five-word comment Matthew tucks into the narrative: "Jesus had compassion on them." The men asked for mercy, and that's just what they got. Jesus didn't heal them because they'd earned it. He simply chose to be merciful.

Most people coming out of abusive situations can't see clearly right away. Accustomed to viewing the world in a skewed manner, they sometimes prefer to remain partially blind instead of making the effort to adjust their perceptions.

In Scripture, freedom and restored sight are often mentioned together:

- "He upholds the cause of the oppressed...
  The LORD *sets prisoners free*,
     the LORD *gives sight to the blind*,
  the LORD lifts up those who are bowed down"
          (Psalm 146:7-8).

- "The Spirit of the Lord is on me,
     because he has anointed me
     to proclaim good news to the poor.
  He has sent me to *proclaim freedom for the prisoners*
     and *recovery of sight for the blind*,
  to set the oppressed free,
     to proclaim the year of the Lord's favor"
          (Luke 4:18-19).

God never desires us to remain shackled by a victim mentality or trapped in distorted thinking. Focusing on Christ's compassion can give us the same boldness the blind men exhibited when they asked for mercy.

You don't even have to wait for Jesus to appear in your fishing boat before you ask him to touch you. You can choose now: healing or disability. Which will it be?

Merciful Lord, deliver me whenever I'm tempted to
succumb to a victim mentality. Thank you for healing me
and setting me free every time I call upon you. Amen.

45

Watered by Encouragement

You gave abundant showers, O God;
you refreshed your weary inheritance.

PSALM 68:9

While taking a tour of the Arizona-Sonora Desert Museum, a woman mentioned that she was growing a potted cactus plant on her apartment balcony back in New York City. Another person on the tour asked how she kept from inadvertently killing it by overwatering.

"I subscribe to a Tucson newspaper," the woman replied. "When the weather page says it rained in the desert, I give my plant a drink."

If I ever move away from my home near Seattle and take native plants with me, I won't have to subscribe to a newspaper to clue me in on their watering schedule. I already know they thrive in continual drizzle.

That's why it took me a while to realize that a little azalea in the corner of my front yard was dying of thirst. It had survived being transplanted from the edge of the driveway during autumn rains. In the midst of April showers the following spring, other bushes I'd also moved were blooming in a happy succession of pinks and purples. But no flowers appeared on the drooping little shrub in the corner. Some of its leaves were even shriveling.

I had no idea why until a rainstorm moved in one day when I was working outside. Every plant in the yard glistened with raindrops—except the smallest azalea. I looked up and noticed that a canopy of three huge fir trees overhead prevented precipitation from reaching anything below.

Most people are like that thirsty azalea. We need showers of encouragement in order to keep from wilting. In fact, we can accomplish amazing feats if someone cheers us on with love and appreciation.

The apostle Paul heartened believers in the early church by "speaking many words of encouragement to the people" (Acts 20:2). He also expressed gratitude to Philemon for following his example: "Your love has given me great joy and encouragement," Paul said, "because you, brother, have refreshed the hearts of the Lord's people" (Philemon 7).

In her book *Your Power of Encouragement*, Jeanne Doering tells of a series of health worries and negative situations that wore her down while in Bible college. "The gloomies hit other students, too," she said. "Talk at meals and prayer cells became a contest of whose problem was the worst. Many professors battled sickness and uncertainties. Finances and a drop in enrollment worried the administration."[1]

Then one chilly morning, a first-period teacher did something that changed Jeanne's outlook. The rookie professor, fresh out of seminary, had been struggling to keep up with lesson preparations in unfamiliar territory. After the morning bell, he asked students for understanding and forgiveness for his poor preparations over the previous few weeks because of an overwhelming workload. Then he requested prayer. Jeanne noticed that his hands shook as he put on his glasses and began the lecture.

The class was stunned. Jeanne and some fellow students decided to take action, and they formed the Barnabas Committee with the purpose of praying for and encouraging that professor and other faculty and staff.

They typed anonymous notes of encouragement, sometimes in silly rhymes, and attached gifts such as candy bars, apples, or animal crackers. Then they sneaked around campus at night to leave the parcels at office doors. They also sent them through the campus mail system, signed "The Barnabas Committee."

When delighted recipients sent the committee thank-you notes in care of the campus post office, the clerk didn't know where to deliver them. Eventually the letters of appreciation ended up in the school bulletin. Soon other people started doing similar acts of kindness. The campus mood turned positive. By concentrating on encouraging other people, members of the Barnabas Committee ended up being encouraged themselves.

Our ultimate example of someone "who gives endurance and encouragement" (Romans 15:5) is God himself. It is he "who loved us and by his grace gave us eternal encouragement and good hope" (2 Thessalonians 2:16). What a wonderful role model for us today!

Just as my sagging azalea perked up when I moved it to a new location where falling rain could reach it, so also people around us respond in wonderful ways when we offer them encouragement. In the process, we will be revived ourselves as waves of life-giving refreshment splash back onto us…even when we're as parched as desert cacti.

Lord, help me to share my words and
deeds of encouragement generously with
thirsty souls around me. Amen.

46

The Good and Bad, the Nice and Nasty

Jesus called the crowd to him and
said, "Listen and understand."

MATTHEW 15:10

As I fumbled coins back into my wallet, the Filipina cashier asked what sounded to me like, "Wahn bah foe meel?"

I enjoy shopping at the international market in a nearby city. It has some of the best prices around. I consider it an adventure to sort through large bins of fruit and veggies to find produce that isn't bruised or wilted. I like saying *hola* to the Hispanic workers, glimpsing foreign-language videos on the Ukrainian deli's TV, and seeing women in burkas select from more than a dozen varieties of rice. I feel as if I'm on an around-the-world tour, except I'm always back home in time for lunch.

But sometimes the English is a little difficult to decipher. Like that day at the checkout stand. I had absolutely no idea what the cashier had said. Figuring she was showing appreciation for my patronage or wishing me a good day, I mumbled "Thank you" and started to collect my purchases. But as I reached for the gallon of milk, she snatched it from me and slipped it into a plastic bag. That had never happened before.

I was halfway to my car before I realized the checker had said, "Want bag for milk?" In this case, misunderstanding had netted me a benefit, but miscommunication doesn't always turn out so well. Like the guy I heard about who got in line at a crowded supermarket and the poor cashier who was having "a terrible, horrible, no good, very bad day." Her register ran out of paper, the scanner malfunctioned, and then she spilled a roll of dimes. When every-thing was finally back to normal and the man's order was rung up, it came to exactly $44.

Trying to encourage the cashier with a cheerful comment, he said, "That's a nice round figure."

The still-flustered woman glared at him. "You're no beanpole yourself."

What do you do when you're nice to people and they misunder-stand? Here's what Jesus said:

> When someone gives you a hard time, respond with the energies of prayer, for then you are working out of your true selves, your God-created selves. This is what God does. He gives his best—the sun to warm and the rain to nourish—to everyone, regardless: the good and bad, the nice and nasty. If all you do is love the lovable, do you expect a bonus? Anybody can do that. If you simply say hello to those who greet you, do you expect a medal? Any run-of-the-mill sinner does that (Matthew 5:44-47 MSG).

Well, as a matter of fact, from time to time I *have* felt I deserved a medal for putting up with nasty people. But these words of Jesus always straighten me out. I don't want to be lumped in the same class as run-of-the-mill sinners. So, I'll choose to pray for people who rub me the wrong way, whether I shop from them, pay taxes to them, or lock my doors to be safe from them. They need my prayers, and I need the discipline of showing grace to those who don't deserve it.

After all, that's what God has done for me. And that makes even a terrible, horrible, no good, very bad day suddenly seem a whole lot better.

> *Lord, help me to remember to pray for others,*
> *even when they misunderstand me. I realize*
> *they need just as much grace as I do. Amen.*

47

Specific Thanksgiving

For this reason, ever since I heard about your
faith in the Lord Jesus and your love for all
God's people, I have not stopped giving thanks
for you, remembering you in my prayers.

EPHESIANS 1:15-16

Before the benefit concert began, a woman walked up to a man wearing military fatigues and said, "Thank you for your service to our country." He looked mystified, but as the woman found her seat in the audience, she knew she'd done the right thing. Later, when her soldier went onstage and was joined by a construction worker, a police officer, and a Native American, she finally realized why he'd been puzzled. She had expressed appreciation to a member of the Village People.

At least she'd been specific when stating the reason for her gratitude. I once received a note on wedding stationery that said, "Thanks for the gift. It will come in very handy." The message was so vague, I wondered if it had been written prior to my gift being opened. I tried to think charitably. At least I'd received a thank-you. Still, a personal touch would have been nice.

Even as I felt guilty for being so picky, the incident caused me to consider how God must feel whenever I offer perfunctory, generic thanks for "blessings that come from Thy hand." I wonder if he turns to the angel Gabriel and asks, "Does she even know which blessings she's talking about?"

The chorus of a classic gospel song many of us grew up with talks about being specific in our gratitude:

> Count your blessings, name them one by one,
> Count your blessings, see what God hath done!
> Count your blessings, name them one by one,
> Count your many blessings, see what God hath done.

The first three verses mention specific times when counting our blessings is especially valuable:

1. when life's stormy billows toss us about and we become discouraged, presuming all is lost

2. when we're burdened with care and the cross we're called to carry is heavy

3. when we see others who are rich in earthly goods but we are not similarly well-to-do

I especially like how the final verse sums up the benefits of blessing-counting:

> So, amid the conflict whether great or small,
> Do not be discouraged, God is over all;
> Count your many blessings, angels will attend,
> Help and comfort give you to your journey's end. [1]

The apostle Paul reminds us to be clear when we thank God so that those around us will be built up in their faith. Otherwise, "how can someone else…say 'Amen' to your thanksgiving, since they do not know what you are saying? You are giving thanks well enough, but no one else is edified" (1 Corinthians 14:16-17).

When we give thanks, we can name everything we're grateful for. Or at least what we have time to mention. Most believers' lives overflow with so many blessings, we'll probably never come to an end of the list. But we should at least try. Being specific in our thanks will encourage everyone around us.

Including all the people in our village.

Lord, thank you for all the blessings I'm
about to enumerate... Amen.

48

Being Grateful for Pig Liver

Whoever eats meat does so to the
Lord, for they give thanks to God.

ROMANS 14:6

During lean times, I economize by using up extra food donated by my family. I'm not fazed by expired best-if-used-by dates as long as soup cans don't bulge or spaghetti packages aren't infested with bugs. Since I don't have to please anyone's palate but my own, I can eat food for fuel rather than for gastronomic pleasure if I have to.

So when Mom generously offered me a grocery bag of food from her freezer, I accepted with gratitude. Its treasures included a Styrofoam tray of rib-eye steak, a warehouse-club-size box of spinach, and some shrink-wrapped pig liver.

I'd never eaten pig liver before, although I grew up enjoying a wide variety of entrées, including venison, grass-fed beef, rainbow and steelhead trout, and an occasional bear roast. Since my father's purpose in hunting and fishing was to put food on the table rather than just enjoy the sport, we found a use for pretty much everything in the animal except the moo—or the growl, as the case may have been.

Many folks today avoid eating liver, the body's filtering system, because of possible residual toxins. Even though it's not my favorite, I couldn't bring myself to throw the liver away, so I thawed, prayed over, and cut up the two small packages. In the process, the liver somehow expanded to fill an enormous skillet. Usually, I freeze extra meal portions to eat later. But I knew that once the cooked liver disappeared into cold storage, I'd never be able to face it again.

So, for the next several days, I steeled myself to thank God for iron-rich protein, and I ate pig liver for breakfast, lunch, and dinner. I confess that during the final meal, I was more grateful for an end of the liver than for the meat itself.

Returning to the freezer to plan my next dinner menu, I ran across a pig heart. *Oh no!* I groaned. *But at least it's not as bad as liver.* Slow-baking the heart in tomato sauce with onions and spices resulted in chunks tender enough to chew—for the next three suppers.

An important key to enjoying life to the full is developing an attitude of gratitude in every circumstance. It helps when I remember all the people worldwide who would be grateful for a plateful of liver or heart. (This has nothing to do with being reminded in my childhood about starving children in other countries who would have appreciated food I didn't want.)

Having had enough of porcine organ meat, I searched the freezer again in hopes of finding something entirely different, such as fish or chicken. Or perhaps ingredients for a vegetarian meal.

That's when the second pig heart turned up, giving me yet another opportunity to practice the discipline of thankfulness.

Dear heavenly Father, I'm grateful for your provisions,
even when they're not what I'd choose. Enjoying
daily life with you is what matters most. Amen.

49

Whenever You Give Alms

Be careful not to practice your righteousness
in front of others to be seen by them.

Matthew 6:1

Financial difficulties had dampened a couple's normally cheerful outlook, but what the husband did on the morning of their wedding anniversary was like a ray of sunshine for both of them. First he awakened his wife and presented her with a beautiful breakfast tray. Then he handed her a single rose, along with a card on which he'd written, "Happy anniversary, my love! In lieu of a gift, contributions have been made in your name to the electric company, our cell-phone carrier, and three credit cards."

It seems that the end of every year includes a season of solicitations. As we're able, most of us enjoy giving to good causes. But finding the right way to give can sometimes be a challenge.

I know of a ministry to low-income families that's swamped every Christmas with offers of decorated trees, holiday meals, and loads of presents. The children and their parents have often been so overwhelmed by the glut of toys, clothing, and electronic gadgets that the ministry finally imposed a dollar limit on what donors could give to each designated family.

One enthusiastic group didn't pay attention to the fine print and applied the dollar limit to each individual instead of to the entire family. The gift pile was so enormous that the small apartment of the group's adopted family nearly ran out of room. The donors probably meant well, but their actions set up expectations that the parents were unable to maintain after graduating from the subsidized program.

What was the real reason for over-the-top giving? Was it to help the needy, or did it simply make donors feel good? Perhaps the desire to receive recognition was also a factor. During his hillside sermon, Jesus explained to the disciples how God wants us to carry out our good deeds:

> Be especially careful when you are trying to be good so that you don't make a performance out of it. It might be good theater, but the God who made you won't be applauding...
>
> When you help someone out, don't think about how it looks. Just do it—quietly and unobtrusively. That is the way your God, who conceived you in love, working behind the scenes, helps you out (Matthew 6:1,3-4 MSG).

I think it's human nature to want a little recognition. But as Jesus pointed out, the godly way to perform good deeds is to do them in a quiet and unobtrusive manner. I know what it feels like when someone does me a favor in order to be recognized and not because he or she is truly concerned about my situation. I don't want to cause anyone else to feel the same way and end up resenting my assistance.

So the next time I have opportunity to help someone out, I'll try to follow the example of the clever and compassionate bill-paying husband—although I can't promise that my charity will extend to breakfast in bed.

Heavenly Father, help me to discern my true motives
for giving. Rather than be driven by the desire
for applause, I want to become mature enough
to care only about your approval. Amen.

50

Driven to Distraction

But Martha was distracted by all the
preparations that had to be made.

LUKE 10:40

As Victoria drove down the freeway one morning headed for work, she noticed a car weaving in the next lane. Pulling even with it, Victoria was alarmed to see the female driver lean so close to the review mirror while applying mascara that her head almost touched the windshield.

Suddenly the car veered in Victoria's direction. It scared Victoria so much, she dropped her own lipstick right into her cup of coffee.

Here in the Seattle area, we know all about driving distractions. Around the time of the winter solstice, our short days are usually overcast, and our nights are depressingly long. You'd think we'd be thrilled every time the sun emerges, but that's not always the case, especially when we're driving. During its short arc across the sky, the sun remains so low on the horizon that rays hit our eyes directly or bounce off approaching windshields in blinding solar flashes. Television traffic gurus alert us to roadways congested by the glare. Fender benders routinely litter highways.

Under those conditions, our primary concern is how to get rid of glaring distractions. That's probably one reason more sunglasses are sold per capita in often-cloudy Seattle than in any other major US city.

No matter how much progress we've made on the road to healing from spiritual, emotional, and other varieties of mistreatment, we can never stop being vigilant against life's distractions. Just making ends meet preoccupies many people. Working extra hours and being involved in money-saving endeavors can leave little discretionary time. Add ongoing caregiving responsibilities, unexpected emergencies, and the extra demands of even joyful occasions, such as weddings, holidays, graduations, or vacation trips, and it can be very difficult to sustain any kind of regular spiritual maintenance.

Those struggles don't make us bad people. They just render us more vulnerable to emotional collisions. God understands. That's why he posts this loving warning:

> Keep vigilant watch over your heart;
> *that's* where life starts…
> Keep your eyes straight ahead;
> ignore all sideshow distractions.
> Watch your step,
> and the road will stretch out smooth before you.
> Look neither right nor left;
> leave evil in the dust (Proverbs 4:23,25-27 MSG).

In addition to regretting the wounds we've suffered, many hurting people also regret the years lost to the situations that inflicted the damage. Those "if onlys" can become major distractions.

But they needn't. Not only does God remind us to set up watch over our hearts and keep our gaze straight ahead, but he also promises to restore what we've lost. "I will repay you for the years the locusts have eaten," he says in Joel 2:25.

The repayment currency is seldom what we expect, but as we guard our hearts against the glare of worry, resentment, bitterness, and other "sideshow distractions," our lives fill with blessings greater than we ever could have imagined.

Now we're less likely to create distractions for our fellow drivers—whether or not they have both hands on the wheel.

Almighty God, thank you for guiding me along the best routes, guarding me against further distractions, and restoring what I have lost. I am very grateful. Amen.

51

Bearing Burdens and Burying Statues

Praise be to the Lord, to God our Savior,
who daily bears our burdens.

PSALM 68:19

Some people believe if they bury a statue of Saint Joseph on a piece of property for sale, the real estate will sell more quickly. So when Katherine was ready to move, she took the Joseph figure from her Nativity set and buried it near her front walk. A few days later, Rachel, a prospective buyer, made an offer. Since Rachel had to sell her home in order to buy a new one, Katherine suggested she also enlist the saint's help.

After burying the statue all over her lawn for a month, Rachel had no nibbles on her house. Disgusted, she tossed the statue into her garbage can by the curb. The following week, a headline in her local paper read, "Town Sells Landfill to Private Developer."

Perhaps Joseph should have remained with the Nativity set.

My daughter has always loved Nativity sets. She's also had a lifelong fascination with nesting dolls. One year I came up with the perfect Christmas gift for her—decorating a crafting kit of blank nesting dolls with a Nativity theme. I'm no artist, and transferring outlines to wooden forms took a lot of time. After I wrestled flat patterns over the curved blanks, I laboriously penciled in lines until I had a fair approximation of each Nativity character.

One of the largest dolls was a camel. I must have retraced and repainted his face at least three times before I was satisfied. That gave me a lot of time to think about the animal's significance. Scripture doesn't specifically mention camels in the events surrounding

Christ's birth, but we assume the Magi rode them on their trek from the East. In any event, we know a camel's purpose was to bear burdens.

While I painted, I thought about how that burden-bearing camel has become a traditional part of the birth story of the ultimate Burden Bearer. Camels are notoriously cranky about carrying their loads. However, not only did Jesus willingly bear the burden of our sins on the cross so we could have eternal life, but he also lifts our burdens in daily life. "Come to me, all you who are weary and burdened," he said, assuring us of his gentleness and humility, "and I will give you rest" (Matthew 11:28).

During the Advent season, traditionally a hectic time for many people, I can think of few blessings more valuable than finding rest and having our burdens lifted. The good news is, we don't have to bury a Christ-child statue to receive those blessings. Jesus himself was buried and rose again to give us life to the full. So, while some may think Saint Joseph helps when negotiating successful real-estate deals, the most important figure in the Nativity account truly is Jesus.

That's enough to make us rejoice any time of the year, even if we're as cranky as camels.

Jesus, thank you for always being ready to lift me
up when I'm bowed down by heavy loads. Amen.

52

Singin' the Blues and Other Forbidden Melodies

Their teachings are merely human rules.

MARK 7:7

When concert pianist Wladimir Jan Kochanski was asked, "Who's your favorite rock group?" he answered, "Mount Rushmore." That sounds like a response I could have given, except I've never been to South Dakota.

My strict upbringing did its best to protect me from rock music—as well as from country music, crooners, big-band tunes, and Motown. In fact, according to my spiritual leaders, unless music was classical or conservatively Christian, it had no redeeming value.

Even mentioning the name of Elvis wasn't allowed. Not only did it rhyme with *pelvis,* but I was expected to know that "true" Christians also understood that rock 'n' roll's evil beat was "straight from the heart of darkest Africa." (That view of Africa is a topic for another day.)

When I played an augmented-fourth piano chord for a devoutly religious music teacher, she scolded me. "Never use that chord in sacred music!" It was years before I learned that the tritone interval it contained, popular in American blues and jazz, was considered by some to be satanic.

It seemed as if my mentors' theme verse was, "I will stop the music of your songs" (Ezekiel 26:13 NLT). I realize now their goal was to limit the sinful enticements of dubious lyrics, sensual rhythms, and negative role models. Nevertheless, the selective blackout left huge gaps in my cultural knowledge. One of those gaps involved Paul Anka's tune "Diana." I had no idea that when I was seven years old, the song bearing my name skyrocketed to number one on Canadian and US music charts. It brought Anka instant stardom and remains one of the best-selling singles ever released by a Canadian recording artist.

Two years ago, a friend teasingly penned these words in a birthday greeting: "I'm so young and you're so old; this, Diana, I've been told."

At first, I took offense. "I'm not old!" I fumed. "I'm upper-middle-aged. I have a lot of good years left!" I didn't realize my friend had adapted his message from Anka's song lyrics. He couldn't believe I'd never heard of the classic rock 'n' roll tune. An Internet search let me know I needn't be offended. The Diana in the song was decades younger than I.

Another cultural-knowledge blackout took place on Sunday, February 9, 1964, when the Beatles made their American TV debut on the *Ed Sullivan Show*. That evening, a record 73 million people tuned in. I wasn't one of them. Our TV set remained off every Sabbath. Even if by some miracle I had been allowed to watch the "ungodly" show, I wouldn't have been home at eight p.m. to see it. We were always at church then.

On Monday morning I learned about the British invasion. Every swooning girl in my eighth-grade class had chosen her favorite member of the Fab Four. Under peer pressure, I picked Ringo Starr at random, knowing nothing about him except his cool name.

Watching news reports about the Beatles was also forbidden, so I strained to decipher songs that blared over my school bus's staticky radio in an attempt to discover what all the excitement was about. My insulation from popular music continued when I entered Bible college, and after graduation, I remained heavily influenced by very conservative family and church members.

In recent years, I've closed some of my popular-music knowledge gaps by watching PBS specials and reading Internet articles. Imagine my shock when I discovered that Elvis Presley had recorded several gospel albums.

I'm not advocating we fill our minds with degrading lyrics, nor should we idolize recording artists. However, if we impose heavy restrictions on people without explaining the solid biblical reasons behind those restrictions, human nature usually rebels. I've seen many overprotected young people indulge in forbidden fruit at their first opportunity and end up more damaged than if they'd been given a measure of guided freedom.

Although by God's grace I didn't rebel, my life has nonetheless been affected by my ignorance of mainstream cultural elements. I know others in the same boat. Overprotected people can't change the past, but we *can* experience peace and contentment by letting go of grudges against overly strict mentors. For anyone who still bears the print of an iron thumb, these three steps may be helpful:

1. Acknowledge that most of our spiritual mentors wanted to protect us, not ruin our lives.

2. Be grateful for whatever benefits did result from the restrictions.

3. Apply the lessons we have learned. At the very least, we can identify more effective ways to help protect those under our care.

When all is said and done, perhaps I'm better off not knowing what Ozzy Osbourne barks at, why Madonna doesn't want Papa to preach, or the nature of Mick Jagger's dissatisfaction. I've come to accept the fact I'll never catch every cultural reference to the popular songs of my lifetime. But who knows? Maybe being unaware of the band Aerosmith until two decades after it formed is an idiosyncrasy that will endear me to my true friends.

Now, I think I'll turn on the stereo and listen to Elvis sing "Just a Closer Walk with Thee."

Lord, thank you for healing me from life's wounds
and for enabling me to let go of any resentment
toward overzealous spiritual mentors. Amen.

Notes

3—Dragging Around Encumbrances

1. Dr. Gregory L. Jantz with Ann McMurray, *Happy for the Rest of Your Life: Four Steps to Contentment, Hope, and Joy—and the Three Keys to Staying There* (Lake Mary, FL: Siloam Press, 2009), p. 127.

8—Like...Fantasy Football Games

1. Romans 12:10; 13:8-10; 1 Corinthians 13; 16:14; 2 Corinthians 8:24; Galatians 5:6,13-14,22; Ephesians 4:2; Philippians 2:2; Colossians 1:4; 2:2; 3:14; 1 Thessalonians 1:3; 3:12; 4:9; 5:13.

2. Hebrews 10:24; James 2:8; 1 Peter 1:22; 2:17; 3:8.

3. 1 John 2:10; 3:10-11,14,16-18,23; 4:7-8,11-12,20-21; 2 John 5; 3 John 6.

24—Creaky Joints and Other Distractions

1. C.S. Lewis, *The Problem of Pain* (New York, NY: Harper Collins, 2001), p. 91.

34—Electrifying Storms

1. Text by Vernon John Charlesworth, 1839–1915.

36—Having Our Cake

1. Agnes C. Lawless and John W. Lawless, *The Drift into Deception: The Eight Characteristics of Abusive Christianity* (Grand Rapids, MI: Kregel, 1995), p. 10.

45—Watered by Encouragement

1. Jeanne Doering, *Your Power of Encouragement* (Chicago, IL: Moody Press, 1985), p. 12.

47—Specific Thanksgiving

1. Text by Johnson Oatman Jr., 1856–1922.

About the Author

Diana Savage has published hundreds of articles, devotions, blogs, and columns. She has written or contributed to more than ten books—including two Chicken Soup for the Soul titles—and has been a professional editor for authors and publishing firms for nearly three decades. She speaks regularly at retreats, universities, and conferences.

For several years, Diana was director of women's ministries at a large West Coast church. She has served in leadership at three writers' organizations, two schools, and a fellowship group for women in ministry. Her humanitarian service includes three years as development officer for a nonprofit ministry to homeless families with children, eight trips to Latin America, and one trip to Nepal and India, where she ministered to girls and young women rescued from forced prostitution.

A fifth-generation Washingtonian whose great-great-grandparents arrived as homesteaders two years before Washington became a state, Diana is accustomed to the misty maritime climate of the Puget Sound. In her spare time, she enjoys cats of all varieties, reading, performing and listening to music, living near her daughter and son-in-law, playing with her grandson, and improving her Spanish.

She is the principal at Savage Creative Services, LLC, a Seattle-area business providing professional writing, editing, and speaking services to clients. Diana earned her bachelor of arts degree from Northwest University and her master of theological studies degree from Bakke Graduate University. She is also credentialed with the National Association of Christian Ministers.

Learn more from her website, www.DianaSavage.com, and her blog, www.heartlifters.net.

To learn more about Harvest House books and
to read sample chapters, visit our website:

www.harvesthousepublishers.com

HARVEST HOUSE PUBLISHERS
EUGENE, OREGON